Journey Into Supermind

JOURNEY INTO SUPERMIND

Unlock Your Inner Potential

RICHARD LAWRENCE

LONDON   NEW YORK   SYDNEY   TORONTO

First published 1995 by Souvenir Press Ltd,
43 Great Russell Street, London WC1B 3PA
and simultaneously in Canada

This edition published 1995
by arrangement with Souvenir Press Ltd.

CN 4790

ISBN 0 285 63252 3 (paperback)
ISBN 0 285 63272 8 (casebound)

Photoset by Rowland Phototypesetting Ltd,
Bury St Edmunds, Suffolk

Printed and bound in Great Britain by
Biddles Ltd, Guildford and King's Lynn

To my wife, Alyson

Acknowledgements

*

With special thanks to John Holder, Patricia Higginson, Alan Moseley and Joan Tarshis for their invaluable help.

Contents

*

Exercises

*

Preface

*

There are no limits to the mind. All of us have the capacity to think, deduce and calculate to the highest degree of rational expression—this is an aspect of the *conscious mind*. We can potentially remember to the minutest detail any and every incident from our lives—this is the process of the *subconscious mind*. We can gain elevated inspiration and deep intuitions, which arise from the *superconscious mind*. These three aspects of mind are at our disposal all the time; it is only a question of how fully we use them.

Some may say that this is all so much theory, that in reality we only have the mental ability we were born with and we just have to make do with that for the rest of our lives. I beg to differ. Admittedly the educational system tends to encourage this kind of pessimism: from our earliest schooldays we are all categorised into different grades of so-called intelligence. I say 'so-called' intelligence because it focuses on a specific use of the brain—a rational approach as opposed to a creative one.

It is now well established that the two hemispheres of the brain govern different aspects of its function—the left-hand side controlling the logical, deductive process and the right-hand side the creative, intuitive process. Both aspects are equally essential, but schooling has tended to emphasise almost exclusively the left-hand side. Higher education, in particular, pours scorn on conclusions achieved through intuitive realisation. The academic will dismiss them as unproven and therefore worthless, but how wrong he is. Many of the greatest breakthroughs in scientific thinking began as inspired ideas. Subsequently they had to be proved logically, but without the initial perception they would never have been discovered. It is said that Einstein's theory of relativity came from a creative daydream; Archimedes had his famous flash of realisation about mass while getting into a bath; James Watt saw the potential of steam while waiting for a kettle to boil, and so on. All these ideas emanated from the creative, right-hand hemisphere of the brain and not through intellectual deduction.

We need to learn to use both hemispheres of the brain in balance. The creative dreamer who cannot manifest his ideas in the realms of practicality can be just as useless as the pure theoretician who has no original ideas of his own. Each of us has a completely unique contribution to make to the world, but one thing is certain: if we do not believe in our potential we have no hope of realising it.

There are many books on the mind which explain in great depth the brilliant chemical and physiological processes of the brain. Others express a multitude of different psychological views, leaving the reader to decide whether he is a Freudian, a Jungian or a follower of some other school of psychology. Scholarly though many of these works are, I do not believe they fulfil the needs of the average person. That is why I wrote this book—to provide a practical method of breaking the shackles of mental limitation which surround us all to some degree. Once you know the shackles are there, you are well on the way to getting rid of them and then moving into the realms of higher mind or, as I have termed it, supermind.

I believe that it is not enough just to provide a few exercises without explaining in detail why and how they work. So I have covered the mind in full—conscious, subconscious and superconscious. The book follows a natural progression which makes it easy to proceed step by step towards whatever goal you wish to attain; you can literally take this as far as you choose. The first part covers the more basic aspects of mind development which are essential to us all—the faculties we need for daily living such as the ability to practise mental relaxation, good concentration, a controlled imagination, an accurate memory and a positive personality. The second part takes you into supermind—a developed intuition, magnetising yourself with natural energies, the radiating of these great powers outwards, and the unlocking of inner mental abilities such as telepathy.

You may wish to control the stress in your life, sharpen your concentration, enhance your imagination, empower your personality, improve your memory, tap into higher mind, develop your intuition or become aware of the natural creative energies which surround us all. You may want to go all the way or only so far. This is a handbook for daily living— virtually a manual for the mind—and my experience of manuals is that the last thing you want is verbosity. You want the information you need put as clearly and simply as possible. Nothing should be missing, but above all, it must be practical and easy to follow.

All the exercises and observations in this book are based on more than twenty years of study, personal experience and the guidance of my first-rate teacher, His Eminence Dr George King, a Western Master of Yoga. It is not intended as a hypothetical work as I do not want to enrich the bookshelves of the world with yet another set of ideas for discussion and debate. It is for you, the reader, to act upon, as far as you choose, in order that you may realise, as never before, the limitless horizons of that extraordinary thing we call mind, and journey into the realms of supermind.

PART ONE

MASTERING YOUR MIND

1

The Starting Point

*

Let's start with the brain, not because it is the be-all and end-all of the mind, but because some people think it is. Even though we use only a fraction of its full capacity, it is almost incredible in its stupendous properties.

THE BRAIN

The human brain operates through numerous interconnecting nerve cells. Brains differ according to their genetic composition, and scientists believe that human nature is determined by our genes. We have brain centres for every sense and muscle group, for moving every part of the anatomy, for distinguishing the sounds of words, facial features and every other sensory response. Thousands of genetic systems are said to have shaped the neurostructure and its myriad complex, interlinking channels.

As scientists delve into the human brain and the enormous bundles of nerve fibres that connect the different nervous centres, they begin to realise just how little they know about its function. As Albert Einstein said, 'The hardest thing to understand is why we can understand anything at all.' Aspects of the function of the brain remain a mystery even to expert neurologists. There is a constant updating of scientific conclusions in this area of study. Recently questions have been raised about the validity of Darwin's theory of evolution: how could the human brain have advanced so much compared to those of our supposed ancestors, the gorillas and chimpanzees? This has never been fully explained by Darwinians.

Interestingly, recent scientific evidence indicates that the brain responds to use and need not degenerate over time. It is said to be the most rejuvenating organ in the body, provided it is used through concentration, memory or some other mental process. What it does not respond well to is neglect. Those people who exercise their mental faculties very little after leaving school, college or work may think their brain is declining with age, when in fact the fault lies in their lack of application. If they make an effort to become more mentally active, they will find that their brain responds quickly and positively.

While conjecture about the function of our neuro-nervous system may be fascinating, it does not really help us to expand the horizons of the mind. Genetics is essential to an understanding of the biological process, but we should never allow our thinking to be limited by it. Never take it for granted that you have inherited certain characteristics and that there is nothing you can do about them. Try to identify your positive mental attributes and resolve to change those you do not want. It would be foolish to ignore genetic inheritance, but hopeless to be ruled by it. For example, I know a young man who believes that he has inherited certain mental weaknesses from one of his parents. Certainly he has the same *potential* weaknesses, but the more he believes them to be an unavoidable genetic fact of life, the worse he becomes and the more he assumes the characteristics he does not want. When he adopts a more positive approach, by attempting to carve out his own destiny and develop a mind of his own, regardless of parental inheritance, he improves greatly. It is useful to understand how your mind works, but you should never be fatalistic about it. As I shall show in this book, we all really do have unlimited potential; it is only a question of how far we decide to take it.

Naturally I exclude from this those who suffer from brain damage or severe mental illness. They need specialised help which is beyond the scope of this book. Having said that, it has been found that positive thinking, and correct breathing in particular, can be extremely helpful in curing some lesser forms of mental illness.

It came as a tremendous shock to philosophers, scientists and theologians when it was first discovered that there was a physical explanation for the mysterious process of thought, which had previously been loosely seen as coming from the soul. Samuel Johnson remarked in the eighteenth century: 'It was never supposed [the poet Imlac said] that cogitation is inherent in matter, or that every particle is a thinking being. Yet if any part of matter be devoid of thought, what part can we suppose to think? Matter can differ from matter only in form, bulk, density, motion and direction of motion: to which of these, however varied or combined, can consciousness be annexed?' The notion of mind existing in matter was astounding to Johnson and his contemporaries, but now we are accustomed to the idea of a physical brain.

As science has discovered that every living thing is composed of cells which are themselves composed of complex but comprehensible chemicals, there has been a tendency to subordinate mind to matter. The assumption is that once we understand the material function of the brain cells and the nervous system, we shall know all there is to know about mind. The pendulum has swung from Johnson's protestations in the eighteenth century to a virtual obsession with material explanations in the twentieth—too far in my view. The whole function of mind cannot be satisfactorily explained by physical laws; we still need metaphysical concepts as well, including the soul if you want to call it that, if we are really to grasp and understand mind.

PSYCHOLOGY

While neurology approaches the mind purely from a physical standpoint, the psychologist attempts to find objective conclusions about mental function through a number of methods. One of the main techniques is statistical analysis, or surveys. For example, Thomas Holmes and Richard Rahe of the University of Washington Medical School performed a study of stressful activities. They investigated five thousand people in the United States from a variety of backgrounds and identified 43 life events or changes that brought about stress. They then compared their findings with European and Japanese statistics in order to determine cultural differences. All found the death of a spouse to be the most stressful event. Death of a close family member was considered far more stressful in the United States and Japan than it was in Europe. Marriage and pregnancy were found to be more stressful in Europe, and going to jail and divorce were rated very stressful in all countries.

Surveys like this are fascinating from a sociological point of view, and psychology is also invaluable in providing research as a basis for psychotherapy and psychoanalysis. But how useful is it really in explaining the function of the mind in everyday life? After all, this is primarily a subjective experience, and while objective data can be a useful source of reference, they do not necessarily tell you about yourself. We are not an approximation or a mean average of a random selection of human experiences, in fact, many of us strive to be the exact opposite. Psychology can give us pointers and expectations, but we must not allow ourselves to be limited by its findings. In a recent radio interview on ESP, I was told by a psychologist that my personal psychic experiences are unproven and invalid because I could theoretically be making them up—in other words lying. Of course I could. But I was not. I knew that; the psychologist did not. So while objective findings have a value, it is subjective experience which will take you beyond the boundaries of your present thinking into something greater.

Before psychology was developed into its current form, people would have sought psychological counselling and advice from a priest, religious leader or spiritual mentor— indeed, many still do. In some cases they would have gone to a tribal elder who was considered to be endowed with wisdom. Now many, in the West particularly, visit their psychoanalyst for advice and, much as they would have done centuries ago, offer their dreams for interpretation. But is this really a step forward? Some would say that advice is better when given by a figure of spiritual or moral authority who is drawing not merely upon an analysis of human behaviour, but upon something of greater worth and merit: an ancient tradition or teaching said to be inspired by a divine force. The answer will depend upon the wisdom of the counsellor in question, but there is no doubt that some of the assumptions we make about the advances of modern science are increasingly being called into question. Paradoxically, at this time of great change there is a hunger for some of the traditional values which got lost in the maze of twentieth-century doubt.

The essential key to manifesting your mind potential is practice. If you want to change your mind power, you have to bring about that change by definite action—not just by studying the constituents of the brain or the behaviour of others. What you do will determine and guarantee your success.

2

Gaining Control of Your Mind

*

It was Sir Winston Churchill who said that the mind never really stops, it only changes. According to modern science, that is true. Scientists measure that change by assessing the frequency of the emission of brain waves.

BRAIN WAVE PATTERNS

No scientist has measured the frequency of brain wave emission from an elevated Master of Yoga entering the highest states of meditation, known as Cosmic Consciousness. For thousands of years it has been claimed that in these states the mind becomes non-existent, as the yogi enters a state of being which is beyond mind. Concepts like this are fascinating and extremely important to the long-term development of mankind, but a long way removed from where most of us are. They do, however, give an indication of what is ultimately achievable, and I shall discuss this more fully in Part Two of the book. For the purposes of this chapter, I shall take it as read that we are emitting brain waves at one frequency or another at all times.

The main instrument used to measure the frequency of brain waves is the electroencephalograph, or EEG, which measures the natural electrical energy of the nerves making up the brain. The electrical voltages generated by the nerves come in waves and the velocity of these waves at any particular time depends on the mental state of the subject.

Four main patterns of brain waves have been classified, each one indicating a different degree of mental activity. They are beta, alpha, theta and delta.

Beta waves are very common among us all and are associated with the state of mind we are in when we are active, alert and engaged in any form of activity, especially if there is pressure involved in it. In this state the peaks are of a low voltage and come at a rate of between 13 and 28 per second.

Alpha waves consist of crests of voltage peaking at a slower rate of about ten per second. These are symptomatic of a person who is awake but relaxed and usually with the eyes closed, so that even visual impulses are blocked from the brain. This is a state often entered into by those who practise basic meditation.

Theta waves are much sought-after by those who wish to enter a higher state of consciousness and these alternate at about three to six per second. They are sometimes associated with people who are asleep and dreaming, but they can occur during periods of particular creativity often associated with a peaceful inner state. Great feats of mind over matter have been performed by those in the theta state of brain wave activity.

Finally there is the delta state, which is the lowest frequency and is regarded as being associated with deep sleep.

A series of tests was conducted in the late 1970s at the University of Tübingen in Germany by Dr Wolfgang Larbig. These used an accomplished Indian fakir who had previously demonstrated the ability to use mind power to endure painful acts without ever experiencing pain. The fakir entered into some form of trance and then, as he had done so many times in the past, thrust metal spikes into his neck and even into his tongue. He exhibited no nervous reaction, apparently, or any evidence that he was experiencing pain. His brain waves were recorded using an EEG and showed that the pattern of frequency emission was the slow theta pattern often associated with dreaming. He was not asleep, but in his state of trance he obviously had the ability to slow down his brain waves. He was able to detach and control the reactions to physical acts which would normally bring excruciating pain. There was no blood emission whatsoever, despite the deep perforations caused in his skin by the metal spikes. Normally these would have left wounds, but in this experiment they only left faint marks.

While I am in no way advocating that we should all set about learning to perform these kinds of demonstration, such as lying on a bed of nails or the numerous other feats which are learnt by some yogis in the East, the story does show that the control of brain wave emission is one of the secrets of mind over matter. It is certainly an indication of the state of consciousness which has been induced.

Such an ability used in another way could bring great powers to the individual, which could be used to help others, not merely as a demonstration of personal attainment. Other experiments have been conducted in various parts of the world and have brought similar results. Sometimes the brain wave cycle shown in these mind over matter demonstrations is alpha rather than theta, but it is never beta.

We all spend too much time in the beta state of mind, and indeed are encouraged to do so by modern social conditions. We are taught at school predominantly to exercise the deductive, rational left-hand side of our brain and to remain mentally busy. We are taught far less to reflect creatively and allow our mind to settle and find its own way under our gentle control. This is in fact what can be learnt from the practice of some form of mental relaxation.

Even the use of imagination is more successful if preceded

by a relaxed state of mind in order to prepare for a creative surge which can come from the force of imagination and inspiration. If you have the ability to concentrate carefully, you can develop the discipline and control that are essential in manifesting the potential of your mind. If you go on to activate the imaginative faculty to bring a balance to the sometimes sterile approach of pure rational deduction and calculation, you will take another step forward and begin to bring a balance to your mental processes. But an essential prerequisite to all this is learning to control the frequency of your brain wave emissions by using mental relaxation techniques, which are sometimes called meditation practices.

As is so often the case, the discoveries of modern scientists lag hundreds or even thousands of years behind the findings of the mystics and yogis. Shri Patanjali is generally regarded as the father of Raja Yoga or the yoga of the control of the mind. His famous aphorisms, which have been published in many translations and are readily available, are the classic text on controlling the mind in order to attain the highest-known states of consciousness. Throughout these aphorisms, Patanjali stresses the need for the cessation of mental activity, sometimes referred to as the 'stilling of the mind'. This process literally means slowing down the emotions and thoughts entering and leaving the brain until you reach the theoretical point of nil.

This, of course, is exactly what scientists have discovered in measuring the brain waves. The alpha state, which is slower than the beta state, leads to a higher degree of awareness and control over material and physical effects; and the theta state leads to a still higher degree of control over mind and matter. Not only did the Indian fakir tested by Dr Larbig completely overcome his sensitivity to pain, he was also able to control the physical reactions of his body, including blood flow, while in the theta wave state which is extremely rarely attained. This type of control over the brain wave frequency can be very useful in life and is not just a means of performing rather sensational demonstrations which simply leave people wondering whether the demonstrator is a freak of nature, a conjuror or really does have some powers.

The only way really to prove to yourself what powers lie within you is to demonstrate them to yourself. There is a wonderful magic within each and every one of us, just waiting to be discovered, but no matter how often we are told this, it will mean nothing unless we experience it first hand. Until then it remains a theoretical possibility.

BIOFEEDBACK

Since the 1960s, a number of researchers have used a system called biofeedback to train people to bring a degree of control to their physical and mental lives. An array of different devices is used to detect and monitor physical and mental activity, including temperature, blood pressure, heartbeat and muscular contraction. The information supplied by this testing is referred to as biofeedback. The idea is that by knowing about these reactions and being able to monitor them as they happen, you learn to gain a certain control over them and start to gain a far better understanding of the mechanisms within you. You are literally getting 'feedback' about your biological self.

Biofeedback sessions may take place in controlled environments, or it is possible to purchase a portable biofeedback device with which to perform your own measurements at home. It is claimed that once the techniques of using the equipment are correctly learnt, there will come a stage when it can be dispensed with—the practitioner will have learnt to gain control over himself without its aid. Of course relaxation, breathing and meditation will still be needed to gain control over these biological reactions but the equipment, the practitioners say, is extremely valuable in monitoring progress. In a sense, biofeedback instruments are just sophisticated mirrors.

YOGA

The ancient practitioners of yoga also monitored their psychological reactions very carefully. It is a little known fact that Hatha Yoga, the system which consists of physical exercises for the purpose of being physically healthy, was originally devised as a secondary system to enhance the higher forms of yoga such as Raja Yoga, Kundalini Yoga and others. It was seen that to be balanced it was important to include physical discipline to be able to enhance and control one's physical reactions, but only as a stepping-stone towards the real goal, which was mastery of the mind. Too many teachers on the mind ignore the interrelationship between body and mind: what affects one automatically affects the other. Advanced practitioners were reputedly able to bring about such a complete state of control that their heart would physically stop beating and they could be assumed, to all intents and purposes, to be dead, when in fact they were in a higher state of consciousness.

In the ancient yoga writings a constant theme is that the key to mastery of the mind is the reduction of the frequency of mind impulses. The Sanskrit word *chit*, which can be translated as 'mind stuff', was looked upon by the pure practitioner of Raja Yoga as something to be removed and cleared away. Another Sanskrit term, *samskaras*, which literally means 'mental impressions', describes thought forms that enter and leave the mind, which can become habitual. These too had to be controlled, reduced in their intensity and ultimately removed. All this has very much in common with the modern discoveries produced by measuring the brain wave frequency and the effects on the consciousness of slowing this down. It is also notable that the slower the brain wave frequency, the more peaceful the individual, and it is in these state of peace, so long as drowsiness or even sleep does not set in, that great realisation can be attained.

Most people are not seeking to learn how to lie on a bed of nails, walk on water or any other such yogic feat. They are more concerned with useful activities. They are going about their business, perhaps bringing up a family, studying at a college or university, helping the community in one way or another or perhaps even the world as a whole to some degree. No matter what your concerns in everyday life may be, the degree of mental control that you have will be absolutely crucial to them all.

STRESS CONTROL

There is a lot of talk nowadays about stress control, and stress is looked upon generally as an evil necessity. Increasingly, people try to avoid stress at all costs. This is not entirely a balanced approach. Stress, by itself, is absolutely essential to all life. In fact, it has been found that the individual who has a void in his or her life, a lack of motivation and a lack of things to do, can become very unbalanced. Many people who have committed suicide were either unemployed or perhaps felt that their lives had no value. They may have been too inactive, there may not have been a large enough stress factor in their lives. The key to dealing with stress is not eliminating it, but controlling it.

There is no doubt that life is pervaded by stress. Even our own conscience can be a form of stress, for if we ignore it, it can come back to haunt us later. That too can be stressful. Certainly the conscience is not something to be avoided, but to be listened to. If we were to take the elimination of stress to its ultimate conclusion, we would be completely amoral people living a life of no responsibility whatsoever and we would certainly not attain the type of fulfilment we seek. On the contrary, people without stress in their lives are the ones who usually end up in a vacuum of despair. Some would say that even such despair is life's way of showing them that there is a purpose.

To change your mind patterns, you need to bring about a change to the function of your inner space. So often people appear on the surface to be changing their viewpoints, when deep inside they do not feel the change at all. This can lead to confusion and all kinds of suppressions. For example, a person may have a strict moral code; he may be the follower of an orthodox branch of religion, whether Christian, Buddhist, Jewish, Hindu, Muslim or any other, and may wish to follow that code diligently. But his natural desires may conflict with that code, which can lead to inner stress and torment. To bring about the required inner change so that his behaviour pattern conforms with his inner desire can be a major undertaking, not just a decision.

Naïve people will often make a pledge or a commitment which they cannot keep because it was not made deeply enough within them. How many alcoholics have taken an oath never to drink again, only to break this oath a few months, weeks or even days later? How many men have promised their wives they will never hit them again, only to fail a short while afterwards? How many people have said they will never lie, but when confronted with a difficult situation take the easy way out by speaking falsehoods? And so on and so on.

How do you really make that change within so that when the time comes to demonstrate your true commitment, your true feeling and belief in that change, you have the strength to do so? There is no easy answer to this; indeed in some ways it is the eternal mystery. However, it is important to feel wholehearted about making the change, and you must also acquire some measure of control over those thought waves which you do not want to inhabit your inner space.

Most people nowadays have demands placed upon them—

far more than they can meet. They are constantly being required to exert themselves mentally for one reason or another. The demands of professional life, family life, of travel, the commendable desire to give something back to the world, to make some charitable contribution to those they have never met—people juggle with these and try to achieve at least some of them. The few minutes a day that might be spent in a simple mental relaxation practice are more than justified by the way the control of one's whole life can be improved.

MIND DEVELOPMENT

One of the secrets of using mind development practices successfully has always been to make them part of your life, not something that you do for five minutes and then forget about. The twentieth-century yogi Dr Shastri taught the need to suspend the lower will, by which he meant the wilful nature that we all have. If one is trying to overcome a particular urge, instinct or desire, Shastri said that we should observe it but not necessarily follow it. In other words, we should decide how we are going to act, not be prey to every passing impulse or feeling that may envelop us from moment to moment. We all do this to a greater or lesser extent; what matters is the actual choice we make.

This also leads us to question who we really are. If we have the ability to choose to suspend our lower will, the lower part of our nature which urges us to behave in certain ways that we don't agree with, who are we then, in reality? We must be something more than our mind if we can choose to suspend an aspect of our mind. By suspending our will, we are starting to tap that superconscious part of our nature which is literally above ordinary consciousness. What exactly is that part of us that is beyond the mind? This is the quest that has preoccupied mystics, metaphysicians and philosophers through the ages—our true identity.

Certain techniques of mind development are designed to take us towards our true identity and are now increasingly being used in all walks of life. Indeed, many companies now run courses in forms of mind development for their executives and trainee managers. They know that an executive who is in a hyperactive state of tension is not in the right frame of mind to make important decisions. He or she needs to operate from a clear space—a cool countenance, if you like. All this means learning to slow down the mind from beta to alpha activity.

Rudyard Kipling's poem 'If' contains many thoughts which are in keeping with the balance produced by mental relaxation and can be associated with the benefits of gaining control of your mind:

> If you can keep your head when all about you
> Are losing theirs and blaming it on you . . .
> If you can dream—and not make dreams your master;
> If you can think—and not make thoughts your aim . . .
> If you can force your heart and nerve and sinew
> To serve your turn long after they are gone,
> And so hold on when there is nothing in you
> Except the will which says to them: 'Hold on!'

To change your mind, you have to do far more than make a sudden decision. You must change your flow of thoughts. You must be determined to suspend the lower will produced by certain impulses and feelings which you do not wish to inhabit your inner space. You must have such a deep commitment to change that, no matter what may arise to test your resolve, you are able to hold on to that inner commitment and merely observe any impulses to the contrary, rather like unwelcome guests. They may float into your mind once, but you can decide that they will never return. In other words, you are starting to determine your type of thought pattern.

Of course, all this takes time and is not easy to achieve.

Gradually, however, you can learn to bring about a balanced and controlled change within your mind, which will give you the ability to switch on and off at will, develop mind control and become more aware of your true identity. The following exercise is a very good way to start this process:

EXERCISE ONE: The Observer

Lie on a hard surface on your back in a physically relaxed state. Your breathing should be as deep and even as possible. Try to observe the thoughts that enter and leave your brain without becoming attached to or involved in them. The purpose of this exercise is to distance yourself from your thought process and hence alter your state of consciousness. It is an excellent preceding practice to other exercises in mind control. It is also very valuable if you are in a state of emotional turbulence or stress, enabling you to gain a better perspective on a particular situation by distancing yourself from it. You should simply observe your mind at work and you will find that issues which you were perhaps seeing out of all proportion fall smoothly into place. Do not rationalise or attempt to resolve any of the thought patterns you observe, just watch them in a completely neutral capacity.

This simple exercise, if practised regularly for a few minutes, will start to bring a change to your mental patterns giving greater control throughout your life, and you will begin to experience the transition from beta to alpha mind wave patterns which will refresh and renew you. The exercise will also help you to become more aware of your true identity—the observer of the thoughts, not the thoughts themselves.

MENTAL DETACHMENT

Much can be learnt about mental detachment from zen philosophy and also from certain schools of martial arts. Stories abound, but two in particular illustrate the value of mind control.

The first of these concerns an exponent of martial arts at an ancient school in China. Contrary to the impressions of some Western people, the true Masters of Eastern mysticism were extremely practical people. They were not idealists who retreated into a world of ideas as some Western philosophers did and still do; instead they saw the need to manifest wisdom in practical and often very simple ways. Swami Vivekananda, who lived in America during the first half of the twentieth century, used to say, when illustrating this need for practicality, 'If you can't cook you can't meditate.' To prove his point, he himself made a practice of cooking for his disciples every so often and, from all accounts, produced an excellent meal!

The exponent of Chinese martial arts could also cook extremely well. He used to demonstrate his ability to pluck a chicken with great speed and skill, much to the amazement of all who beheld him. He became well known for this. One day one of his students asked him exactly how he had learnt to perform this feat. He replied that the secret was that he did not perform it. What he meant by this simple statement was that through his expertise in the martial arts he had learnt to detach from his basic thought pattern and contact a higher part of his nature. This higher nature could take over any action he performed, including plucking a chicken.

The second story often causes surprise among people who hear it. They are mystified because they do not really understand its meaning. It concerns a student of a zen master who used archery as a system of personal development. Behind martial arts, archery, swordsmanship and so on, there is a much higher purpose. In the original martial arts schools these skills were not taught for the purposes of combat or even self-defence, but to develop lightning-like reactions at a mental level and the mind control that is required to bring these about. This zen master expected his students to achieve perfection in archery—only when they had done so would they be released from school as having passed his test, and they would then receive the status that went with that.

One student was truly excellent in his archery skill and was able to get a bull's eye every time from a considerable distance. Every so often he would be required to demonstrate this to his zen master who was the only person who could pass him as having qualified the test of the school. Time and time again he demonstrated this feat to his master, getting bull's eye after bull's eye, but each time the master said, 'No, you are not ready yet. You will have to practise some more and come back.' Eventually he reached the point where he was so frustrated that he was ready to walk out of the school in disgust and no longer cared whether he got a bull's eye or not. After all, his evident skill did not seem to have any effect upon the master or lead him to qualify to leave the school with full honours. At his final test, in virtual disregard of the rules, he aimed his arrow, pulled his bow, and let go without concern for hitting his target. The arrow was slightly off centre. Much to his amazement the zen master was full of glee and congratulated him warmly, saying, 'Now you have passed the test.' He was then released from school with full honours.

What was the message the zen master was trying to give to his student? He wanted to teach him that it is one thing to attain a degree of mastery over an action, but that full mastery is not gained until you detach from the action itself. The student was far too attached to gaining a bull's eye and the sense of pride and satisfaction that went with it. His frustration led him to detach from the results of his action, which the zen master could then see. Of course, had he not already proved that he could attain the bull's eye at will, the master undoubtedly would not have passed him as being qualified. But he was not satisfied with the degree of mental detachment his student had attained and would not release him from the school until he had proved this also.

This lesson may seem very subtle and obscure to many of us in the West, but a great teaching lies behind it. In a world where people are constantly seeking to improve their material lot, the person who becomes too attached to the result of his actions is also the one who may be prone to the greatest loss. For example, in industry a businessman may be extremely successful and become very attached to his acquisitions and success, but when disappointment strikes, maybe due to factors beyond his control, he may suffer great stress, possibly heart disease, and will therefore no longer be able to continue in his business. How successful has he really been as a businessman?

In the world of show business a performer can become very attached not so much to the performance as to the accolades she receives afterwards. Then, when she experiences a bad period of unpopularity in her career, she goes to pieces and her performance also falls apart. She is virtually like a balloon that has been burst and she has nothing left to give. But the performer who is more concerned with mastering his performance, and less with the results in terms of applause or financial reward, will continue to work on the craft of performing and is more likely to survive the troughs in his career.

The same is true in family life. All parents go through periods of concern about their children and their children's progress in school or social life. If parents see their children as an extension of themselves and take pride before others in their success, they will be deeply embarrassed and crestfallen when their children do badly or behave badly, not so much for their children but for themselves. If they care only about the children and not about the effect their behaviour may have on their own image, they will be much better parents and will continue trying to help their children as much as they can. Of course, ultimately no parent is completely responsible for the outcome of her child. Those, like myself, who believe in reincarnation acquire a certain detachment about many things. For example, a parent who believes in reincarnation will realise that her child has already gained many attributes before he was born, and she will not therefore feel entirely responsible for the way he turns out.

Sometimes, in an extreme case, a child may show villainous tendencies even at a young age and may commit horrendous acts. Because of the conditioning of some psychologists and sociologists, parents are made to feel completely responsible for this. They are told that their children are solely the products of their genetic inheritance and the environment in which they live. Although these two factors are very important, the reincarnationist believes that they are not the only considerations. Parents have a responsibility and a commitment to bring up a reincarnating soul in the best way they can, but the knowledge that their child is not totally a product of themselves gives them a degree of mental detachment. After all, you can see that children have certain character traits, certain inherent knowledge about human nature and about life, which you have not taught them. It may offend some parents to be told that their children are not totally the product of themselves; others, however, will find that it makes a lot of sense and gives them a broader perspective on parenthood.

A certain mental detachment, by the way, should not make you a cold person. Mental detachment and love go hand in hand. After all, if you have no ulterior motive for your affection for others, you are able to give a much purer form of love than if there are conditions attached. If there is something you want back, if there is a certain selfish desire that you want fulfilled from a particular relationship, then the relationship and the love you can give are limited to that degree. This is one of the first things you realise in forming a successful relationship. Ultimately, the most powerful love you can give is that which has no conditions attached.

MENTAL RELAXATION

By developing mental detachment you will be able to relax your mind and benefit throughout your life; it will be available to you whenever you want it. This does not mean that you will no longer care about the world—that is not the sort of detachment I am talking about. Nor will you care less about those close to you—in fact you will be capable of caring more. But you will be able to switch on and off far more easily than you have in the past. This is an attribute that is crucial to successful living and is one of the keys to unlocking your inner potential.

One of the best ways to relax the mind and overcome stress imbalances is to practise rhythmic breathing. The more even the breath, the more even the brain waves. Ancient Hindu philosophy saw the whole of life as one breath. The out-breath brought about manifestation and the in-breath returned manifestation whence it came. There are numerous books available on diet, encouraging us to eat and drink correctly. This is a very important factor, and indeed the way we eat and drink will also have an effect on the way our mind operates. But far more important than diet is correct breathing and there are not nearly so many books available on this subject.

In order to start to relax your mind it is extremely beneficial to learn not only to harmonise the out-breath and the in-breath in rhythmic cycles, but also gradually to lengthen them. The following exercise can be used to do this:

EXERCISE TWO: Harmonising the Breath

Experts in the science of breathing, known in the East as *pranayama*, stress that the length of a person's breath should not be forced. Each of us should be allowed to develop this gradually in our own time. The pressures of life, however, are such that we spend a lot of our time in very shallow breathing. In this and all subsequent exercises you should breathe through the nostrils.

For this exercise you should be seated on a hard-backed chair with your spine erect, but without tension. If you know a suitable yoga *asana* (posture), you can use that instead. On the in-breath, visualise the trunk of your body as a tumbler being filled with a pure white fluid. As you breathe in through the nostrils, the tumbler is being filled from the bottom of the trunk, through the abdomen, the stomach, the chest, right up to the shoulders, with this pure white fluid, until at the end of the breath it is completely full. Allow the abdomen to swell outward somewhat on the in-breath and make the breath as long as you possibly can without strain. On the out-breath, empty the glass from the top of the shoulders downwards. Pull the diaphragm in slightly on the out-breath without force and empty it to the very bottom of the trunk in the exact reverse way as you did on the in-breath.

Continue this in-breathing and out-breathing with the mouth closed, filling up the tumbler and emptying it each time as you do so. When you are able to do this without too much effort and the visualisation becomes natural to you, start gradually to lengthen the in-breath and out-breath. It is very important that you maintain the rhythm between the in-breath and out-breath and that you extend them both equally. Remember that the same tumbler that you filled has to be completely emptied.

This simple exercise will not only start to relax your mind but will also bring you a feeling of well-being, and if you do it for a few minutes every day you will be amazed at the rejuvenation and refreshment you feel. You will start to feel a greater inner peace coming into your life and, as well as mental clarity, this is very good for your physical health.

There are many systems which can be learnt to develop the kind of physical control that will enable you to relax the physical body more or less at will. Systems like T'ai-Chi, certain branches of Hatha Yoga and some of the martial arts, such as Aikido and Kung-Fu, can bring about an immense control to your physical reactions. This in turn will develop your ability to relax the nervous system very quickly and hence slow down the motion of brain waves from the beta state into the alpha state and possibly beyond.

Below is a simple exercise you can do to help mental relaxation. Some of the simplest exercises are in fact the most effective, provided they are practised diligently, and this one will work for you particularly if you do it when you feel nervous and tense. Of course, very often moments of tension are also inconvenient times to do practices. One particular school of Buddhism used to instruct its students, at any given moment, to stop whatever they were doing and become mindful of themselves and their feelings. If you are able at a moment of great tension to discipline yourself actually to stop your activities, provided it is possible to do so, and perform this relaxation exercise, you will find you start to develop, at will, a greater physical relaxation which in turn will increase your mental relaxation and your ability to control stress.

EXERCISE THREE: Relaxing the Mind

To do this you ideally need to be in a room where you can close or lock the door so that no one will interrupt you. It may be helpful to play some very soft and gentle music. New Age music is particularly good for relaxation techniques because it tends to be devoid of strong emotions. You can find a New Age Music section in most record shops nowadays. You do not want a piece of music with strong melody or passionate harmonic progressions, which will involve your mind and distract you from the relaxation practice you are going to perform. While classical music is extremely powerful and uplifting, it is often intellectually complex and demands the active involvement of the thought processes, which you do not want for this exercise. Rock music is the exact opposite of what you want because of its emotionally stimulating content. The lights in the room should be dim and you may find it conducive to light some incense or use incense oils to produce a calming environment. Again, you do not want a very strong smell but one which relaxes you and perhaps has positive associations for you, such as sandalwood.

You then simply lie on your back on the floor and start to practise rhythmic deep breathing. Close your eyes and instruct yourself gently to relax. After all, it is the brain which gives signals to the nervous system in the body, causing all movement and all physical action. In this simple exercise you are controlling the instruction and making a gentle request to your nervous system to relax. Be absolutely confident that this relaxation will take place, have no doubt in your mind, and you will find that gradually it will indeed happen. On the first occasion you may or may not be successful in inducing a relaxed state, but if you persist you will gradually gain control over the tension in your body and mind and this can have a major change throughout your whole life, especially for people who suffer from hypertension or nervous conditions. It is a harmonising practice which can lead to a deep state of mental relaxation. Try to avoid drowsiness or sleep because you will lose the benefits of this practice by doing so. What you are trying to attain is a relaxation at will, when you are still fully conscious.

This exercise may seem absurdly simple on the face of it, but what you are really doing is isolating the stress and tension you feel by focusing on it and then changing it into a condition of relaxation. You are telling your body who is boss and bringing about a controlled relationship between your conscious mind and your subconscious nervous reactions. By doing this regularly, you will find that you gradually learn to switch your tension on and off at will, even at times when you are not doing this practice. Do not be put off if it does not seem to work at first; it may be that you have developed stress and tension over a period of time and your nervous system is not used to this kind of gentle but firm instruction.

Persist with the exercise and gradually you will find that it starts to work, thereby affecting your whole life. You are gaining control over your stress responses and showing your subconscious and bodily reactions that you are in charge. This will bring about a sense of peace, because this is what the nervous system really wants, it does not want to drive a rudderless boat. In this exercise you are virtually starting to take the helm and determining the direction and speed at which you intend to move.

MIND CONTROL

Once you are aware of the changing patterns of your mind and have started to practise mental relaxation exercises, you are in a position to move on to techniques of mind control.

You are the master of your mind, and its tremendous power is at your disposal, just waiting to be activated. Many organisations exist to teach one method of mind control or another. Some of them are very helpful but others, to put it politely, are counterproductive and have taught unbalanced methods which, in the long run, have not helped the individual at all.

Discrimination is therefore vitally important and there are certain criteria that need to be looked for if you wish to develop control. For example, you should not practise a technique that encourages overt suppression of your basic thought patterns. Very advanced schools of yoga used methods of suppression at certain stages, but only under the strict control of teachers and then only with students who were intent not so much on just improving their minds, but upon attaining the highest states of mystical awareness known on earth. The average person needs a safe, balanced method which does not force the mind in any particular direction, but gently allows its function to come under the control of the practitioner. Crucial to this is the slowing down of the frequency of the brain impulses.

The best way to do this is by using meditation techniques, but let me first say a word or two about the word 'meditation'. This word is bandied about by many different people to mean many different things. Some will use it to mean some high and elevated state of consciousness in which great powers are gained by the practitioner, known in Sanskrit as *siddhis*. But most people nowadays really mean some form of mental relaxation exercise—in other words, an exercise which will take us from the very active beta state of mind into the more contemplative alpha state.

We all do this sometimes, and it is a good thing we do because the alpha state of mind is much better for our health. It decreases tension, clears up psychosomatic ailments, reduces disease caused by stress, lowers our blood pressure, strengthens our immune system, and some say it even slows down the ageing process. The rate of oxygen consumption decreases by between ten and 20 per cent and, very importantly, lactate concentration in the blood also decreases when we start to move from the beta into the alpha state. Apart from all this, it is a very pleasant thing to do.

Of course, we all need the stimulation of mental activity, but as in all things, an excess is not good for us. In today's world there is an excess of beta consciousness. The impulses of the media, news, advertising and entertainment are all geared mainly to beta activity and less time is spent in gentle country pursuits and relaxed living. Relaxation is now sought through increased activity and stimulation rather than less. All this means that alpha living is becoming a rare commodity, which is one more reason why it so important to learn some mental relaxation techniques to bring about this change of consciousness and start to give you the ability to control it in your everyday life. By doing these exercises you will learn through personal experience what it takes to bring about this change, and gradually you will become able to achieve it more at will and when you choose. Here is one exercise you can try.

EXERCISE FOUR:
From Beta to Alpha Consciousness

Sit on a hard-backed chair with your hands facing palms downwards on your knees and your spine erect. Do not slouch, but try to be as physically relaxed as possible, especially around the neck and shoulders. If there is some tension in these areas, gently rotate your neck, first in a clockwise then an anti-clockwise direction. Do not force this, or you might exacerbate the tension, but just allow the neck to roll round, first one way then the other, and gradually the tension will slip away. Keep your eyes closed throughout and start by observing your thoughts as you did in Exercise One, The Observer.

Gradually you will remove yourself from the thought process and become the observer, as you did before, but this time go one step farther and observe not only your thoughts but also your feelings. As a particular thought process enters the brain it may carry with it certain associations. For example, if an incident which occurred in the past floats into your mind, it may carry with it some emotion, such as anger, frustration, elation or disappointment. Attempt to smooth out these emotional reactions by observing them in a detached light during the exercise. This is a very useful thing to be able to do in life. Even if you ultimately decide to act upon your feelings, it is always beneficial to be able to distance yourself from them first, in order to make a clear decision. It will also enable you to discriminate between an inner, intuitive feeling and basic emotion. The two feelings are virtually chalk and cheese, yet we do not always realise it at the time.

So, in this practice, observe both the thoughts entering your brain and your emotional reactions to these thoughts. Let the thoughts go and try to smooth out the emotions by distancing yourself from them. Observe them but do not attach to them. You will find that, providing you do not force them under, but just watch them, they will disappear, either instantaneously or gradually. You will reduce the level of turbulence within you as well as the attachment to thought processes, and this will help you to move from beta to alpha consciousness.

In neither this nor any other exercise should you attempt to blank out your mind. You are conscious, you are aware, but you are observing as opposed to becoming actively involved in your thoughts and emotions. This exercise will benefit your physical health, and it will bring you a clearer perspective on your whole life and the direction you are taking. You should certainly experience this effect after several weeks of regular practice.

In order to bring about mind control you need to be able to move from a state of 'doing' to a state of 'being'. You may find it easier to think of it as 'living in the now'. If our minds are always focused on what we are going to do next and what we did in the past, we shall not gain the full benefit of experiencing the now. This type of concept is fundamental to learning mental relaxation techniques, which are designed to take us more and more into the now, more and more into a state of being rather than doing. As we slow down the brain waves from the beta state into the alpha state, we increasingly reduce the process of thinking consciously and replace it with a more direct sense of awareness of existence.

Another key to achieving this state of mind control is always to focus on your true identity or real self. In other words, you should become the thinker, not the thought process itself. Too many people identify with their thoughts and think that they are those thoughts, that their character is composed of the thoughts that go through their mind. On the contrary, we have an identity beyond thought. We are the person who chooses our thought process and this is the real key to gaining control over our mental faculties.

AFFIRMATION

Eastern philosophy found the key to control by concentrating on what was termed the 'I am presence'. Affirmations were devised in a number of languages, using the words 'I am'. 'I am the master of my mind and my body' would be one such affirmation which the student would repeat mentally hundreds or even thousands of times a day, until he started to detach his identification from the thought process and become the controller of the thought process instead. Spiritual affirmations such as 'I am the divine presence' were used by some because it was believed that within each and every one of us is a divine spark of God. This concept may offend some religious belief systems, but really, in essence, it is the most positive affirmation you could possibly make. By saying this, you are developing divine attributes of perfection, such as pure love and so on.

The mystic would say that the true nature of self is divine, that it is only our ignorance that stands between us and our real self, and that this ignorance is our attachment to the thought processes that go through our brain in waves. We need to control our minds in order to discover our true identity as the controller of our thoughts. If this idea seems rather frightening, suggesting that you are in danger of losing your true identity, rest assured that with a carefully balanced approach this will not happen. After all, you are really saying that in your innermost being is a seed of perfection, and through practising affirmation you are trying to contact this seed so that it can grow and blossom throughout your personality which itself is manifested through the expression of your mind.

In the practice of affirmation you are constantly trying to improve yourself and gain control over your self. Providing you maintain a balance and always remember that all of us have a long way to go, then spiritual affirmations such as 'I am the divine spirit' will be extremely valuable to you. They should always be performed with due reverence, and if you are not a believer in some form of divinity it would be better not to practise them at all. If something is done without real belief, it cannot work effectively for you.

By practising such affirmations regularly you will start to develop greater self-confidence. As a balance it is also a good idea to reflect upon your weaknesses so that you can resolve to improve them. This kind of examination can be difficult, but if done carefully it will be extremely rewarding. The best way to approach it would be to start with an honest self-examination and follow with the practice of affirmation. If you would rather not use a spiritual affirmation, then simply use one such as 'I am the master of my mind and body'.

By practising both the honest self-examination, which is virtually a personal confession, and the positive affirmation, a very powerful balance will be created in your life. The confessional procedure as adopted by the Roman Catholic Church has its roots in a very ancient practice, predating Christianity by hundreds of years, which involved cleansing oneself through complete admission of one's failings. This is not easy to do, and if you do find it easy, then you are not doing it properly. There is no need, however, to do it with anyone else present unless you really want to. If it is followed by a very positive practice, such as affirmation, then you will have the complete balance.

Where the Roman Catholic Church has gone wrong from the point of view of mental balance is by focusing too heavily on people's failings and guilt and not enough upon their inner strengths. The exclusive emphasis on the need to seek forgiveness of your sins can lead people to believe they are not capable of overcoming these failings themselves. My intention here is certainly not to criticise the Roman Catholic religion, as I have respect for all religions. Some, of course, are more powerful than others in terms of personal development, but they all have very valuable gifts to offer. In some cases they also have imbalances in their teaching and, from the point of view of mind development, it is sometimes necessary to note these.

CHANGING YOUR MIND

To summarise what we have discussed in this chapter, mind development is like a double-edged sword. On the one hand you are a person of human failing, frailty and weakness, but on the other you are in your true nature completely divine. You have all strength, all power and all wisdom at your disposal in the magical recesses of your inner self. If you realise both these things simultaneously, in a way that is gentle with yourself, then you can start to master your thoughts and tread the road to full mind control.

Some teachers refer to the lower self and higher self in order to explain this dichotomy. You have this inner potential, this fantastic power within, and you also have a more basic nature which is composed of the various desires, impulses, thoughts and feelings which enter your being sporadically, almost haphazardly at times. The journey of mind control is to raise the level of these sporadic impulses onto a higher level of being. Then you will discover your true identity.

Another key to gaining the confidence to practise mind control is a philosophy which governs many branches of Buddhism and other schools of metaphysical thought. Simply put, this states that we are all inherently enlightened but that we do not realise it. It is not so much a question of gaining enlightenment, but of realising that it is already here.

It is quite amazing what realisation can do. There are many extraordinary cases, in both World War I and World War II, of people who were severely injured but did not realise for some time what had happened to them. In the heat of battle, with adrenalin flowing through them, they did not feel any pain. There are even extraordinary cases of soldiers who, for example, had a leg blown off and were able to continue running for some time until they looked down and saw that there was no leg there; then they collapsed in anguish and pain. I met a war veteran who told me he was once severely injured and did not realise until much later that a shell had penetrated his back. Because of this he felt no pain at all, and although he saw some blood dripping down, he did not know where it came from. This is a combination of not realising what had happened and the excitement caused by the rush of adrenalin through the nervous system.

In bringing about mind control, it is also essential to bring in its wake some control to the nervous system. The flow of adrenalin, and of noradrenaline, its counterpart, are absolutely vital to our bodily function. The secret is to keep this flow in balance and under control. It is certainly true that the inspired individual requires some flow of these substances in order to be elevated. The balanced control of them causes what is known as the 'fight-or-flight' response. The fight response is to rise up to a challenge, to be activated and to want to express yourself. The flight response is to want to go within yourself, to be quiet, to retreat from activity. Both of these have their place in our lives.

Some medical researchers believe that if we can understand the flow of adrenalin we shall also understand the secret of addiction. For example, they postulate that a gambler is someone who associates the surge of adrenalin that he gets from gambling with the gambling itself. It is not actually the gambling that he is addicted to, but the surge of adrenalin he gets from the activity, since adrenalin is a chemical which is released into the system, which has addictive properties. The same would apply to many other activities.

Workaholics become addicted to the adrenalin release they get from their work; even some sporting activities can become addictive, as 'golf widows' will confirm. As with stress, it would be entirely wrong to eliminate this flow of adrenalin. We need it, we require it, but we do have to learn to acquire control over it, and one of the keys to this is realisation. If the gambler realised that it was not the gambling itself that he was addicted to, but the surge of adrenalin he got from it, then he might look elsewhere and overcome his addiction. He might be able to find another way of releasing the adrenalin, so gradually controlling this addiction.

This is why so many people who were addicted to drugs have found meditation exercises to be a key to 'curing' them. Through these inward-looking practices, which start to bring balance and control to the inner urges and the flow of adrenalin within their psyche, they are able to handle the addiction at its root source.

Even if you are not troubled by any form of addiction, you may still wish to change your perspective and priorities in some aspect of your life. You can do this by gaining control of your mind. The next step is to overcome any and every obstacle in the way of a full expression of the fantastic mental potential at your disposal. The following chapter explains how to do this.

3
The Art of Positive Thinking

*

Positive thinking is an essential ingredient for success in all aspects of life. It is the most immediate and obvious result of practising mind control. The successful entrepreneur has a positive approach to a line of commerce and sees it through to success. The successful sportsman develops his skills and relentlessly determines to overcome his weak points through concentrated positive effort. A successful philosopher has such a positive belief in his own powers of thought, and focuses his concentration so intently and unerringly, that he is able to make certain deductions about the purpose and nature of life. The scientist, the gardener, the housewife, the schoolchild, the musician—no matter what field of life you turn to—the secret of success is always a positive approach to whatever you tackle.

CONCENTRATION

Hand in hand with positive thinking is the ability to practise single-minded concentration. This is absolutely vital, because without it, no matter how positive you may be, you will waver in the goal you seek. Therefore, in order to practise positive thinking it is necessary to learn effective concentration.

All of us learn to concentrate to some extent in school and throughout life, but if we are really honest, our minds are all too often like grasshoppers. Some methods of study are highly convoluted and attempt to force the mind into unnatural patterns in order to learn—the image of the absentminded professor is more than just a music hall joke. Some forms of academic endeavour, which cause the brain to excel in a certain field, are nevertheless so unnatural as to bring an unbalanced reaction like absentmindedness. The acid test of concentration is often the success of the individual in a very practical endeavour. It is no good being able to think about complex academic formulae if you cannot do something simple like cooking a meal or driving a car. Of course, if you have a physical disability this does not apply, because then the problem is obviously not a result of lack of concentration on your part. No matter what goals you set yourself for mental improvement, none of them will be achieved without a successful degree of concentration.

So how do you go about improving your concentration? Your first task is to become aware of the function of the conscious mind. A good analogy is the radio-receiving set: waves of thought are transmitted through space and detected by the tuner which is your brain, and the type of thought-waves you attract will depend on your mental or emotional state at the time. The key to the practice of concentration is not to employ force. All too often in school children are taught to strain their minds, and this can easily be seen by observing the tension and stress that they undergo in examinations and at certain types of class work. For example, there are certain mathematical formulae which are highly complex and require advanced deductive abilities. While this may be absolutely essential, and indeed very important in certain educational fields, it is not entirely balanced to focus exclusively on this type of work. It is necessary also to exercise the imaginative side of the brain, which ranges more freely and in a less constrained way.

True concentration focuses the whole of the brain, both the right and left hemispheres.

The way to start doing this is by allowing the conscious mind to function fully. The word 'allow' is a key one in learning concentration. If you try to force the mind without first allowing it to function in its own way, you will not successfully gain control over it. If you regard the mind as a wild horse which needs to be trained, you can see the difference between forcing and allowing the conscious mind to work. To force it would be to harness the horse and forcibly drag it by the reins around a field. This way the horse will never learn to run in a controlled way of its own volition. To break a horse, the horseman rides on it, allows it to try to buck him off, but takes control through careful handling of the reins and teaching the horse to respond to him.

You first need to practise the simple exercise of watching your mind at work, as in Exercise One, The Observer. You should observe your thoughts and feelings as they float into your brain, like the receiving set on the radio. Do not attempt to change them at first, but just observe what goes in and out, as if you were one step removed from the process. This is easier said than done and takes practice, but after a while you will find that you get to know your mind, and only by getting to know it will you be able to control it.

When you have done this for a while, you must go on to the next step. If you did nothing but watch the process of the mind you would not learn to concentrate. Using the analogy of horse and rider, this is only a preliminary stage to enable you to take your seat on the horse and gradually pull in the reins.

The next stage is vitally important. You introduce a concentration into your mind as a focus. This should be a balanced exercise which uses both sides of the brain. If you decide, for example, to recite a positive mental suggestion, such as, 'Every day in every way, I am getting better and better', you should try to do it with feeling, otherwise it will just be a rather cold, intellectual exercise and will not have the potency you need to learn successful concentration. You should say it for at least five minutes at a time, out loud, with all the conviction you can muster; then you will gradually start to feel better.

POSITIVE SUGGESTION

Positive thinking is something which you can introduce into your life and thereby change it for the better: you will notice the effects immediately. There are always two ways of looking at things—positively or negatively, with optimism or pessimism. I am not advocating an unrealistic approach—that you should become a dreamer without any firm foundations. You do not need to do this to develop the art of positive thinking. You simply need to focus on the most positive aspects of any given situation. The old adage, 'difficulties were made to be overcome', may sound like a cliché, but it is an extremely useful approach to life.

Positive suggestions definitely help with this. If you think strongly enough, 'I am going to get better', you will cultivate a frame of mind in which improvement takes place. If, on the other hand, you expect to get worse, it is likely to happen. This is not just an old wives' take but a well-proven fact—try it and you will find out. The same applies to any aspect of your life. If you have a very difficult examination or job interview, a positive approach can make all the difference. It will be no substitute for study and essential preparation but it can take you a long way, helping you to radiate a self-confidence which could prove decisive. If you believe in yourself, you are more likely to draw on your own potential than if you do not.

There is a vast difference between positive thinking and self-delusion. For example, if you are ill, do not kid yourself by thinking 'I am not ill'—this could make you worse. You are then practising a form of denial which does not work. But do think, 'I am going to get better.' This is a positive suggestion and will feed your subconscious mind with the thought pattern it needs to help you get better. That is why it works.

You can use specific concentration exercises to improve your positive approach to life. Many examples of these can be found in books, but the hallmark of a good one is that it contains positive thoughts and feelings throughout. The mind likes to work with the positive; this is far more natural to it than negativity. The more beneficial your concentration exercise is to all life, the more in harmony you become with the whole, which will enhance your concentrative abilities even further. An exercise which is beneficial to yourself and to others will virtually act as food for your whole being. If you do a negative visualisation it will do harm, for there is a power to all thought, but the person you will harm the most will be yourself: sooner or later the thought you put out will return to you.

Therefore you are looking for concentrations, meditations or visualisations which are in every way positive and beneficial. Since this is a practical book, designed to help you release your inner potential, it will be far more useful if I give you some specific examples that you can use yourself. The following have proved very effective for me and I am sure will work successfully for you, if you apply your concentration to them.

EXERCISE FIVE:
Concentration for Good Health

Make sure, as in many of these practices, that you are seated comfortably on a hard-backed chair or in a conducive yoga *asana* if you know one, with the back straight and without any tension in the shoulders or neck. Your hands should be placed lightly on your knees. Start by practising deep, rhythmic breathing. This will induce a calmness into which you can introduce your visualis-

ation. After a few minutes, begin to concentrate on the whole of
your body and, as you do so, go through each part of your anatomy, visualising it as being in good health. Where there may be
an ailment in your body, do not concentrate on the ailment at all
but visualise radiant health in its place.

This is an extremely simple exercise, yet one which can work
for you very effectively indeed. You are virtually planting into
your subconscious mind, through using your concentrative and
imaginative powers, a concept of good health. This principle has
been used in the past to bring recovery from illness and disabilities
which were considered to be beyond recovery.

EXERCISE SIX:
Concentration for Physical Relaxation

This exercise is very similar to the last one except that your goal
here is to induce a state of physical relaxation rather than radiant
health. This is sorely needed by many people in the world today,
who suffer from the many nervous strains of modern living—
some of which are subtle and others very obvious. It is a good
exercise to do particularly if you are highly strung or in a very
anxious state.

Again, start by adopting the comfortable position described in
the last exercise and practise deep, rhythmic breathing. If you
are in a very nervous state this may be difficult to do, but it will
be all the more important for you to persist. Always keep the
mouth closed in these breathing exercises and gradually start to
make the out-breath and the in-breath as even as you can. Having
done this, concentrate on each part of your anatomy, as you did
before, but this time, instead of visualising it in radiant health,
visualise it in a state of peace. You can virtually encourage your
anatomy to relax by talking to it. Some people will say to their
legs, for example, 'Relax, legs.' Others will just prefer to visualise
this relaxation process taking place. You can go through your
body from top to bottom and back again and you will start to
feel a great peace envelop you.

Again, this is a very simple exercise, in which you are
instructing your subconscious and gently guiding it to bring about
that natural state of relaxation which eludes so many of us. If
you do this exercise regularly, you will gradually learn to bring

about physical relaxation in any part of the anatomy you choose—a most valuable ability in life.

These two exercises in concentration are not only practical and useful in daily living, but they also illustrate one of the most important aspects of releasing the power of the mind— the intensive use of your faculty of concentration. The secret of success is to have a positive and definite mental image and never to allow it to get out of control. For this you need the discipline provided by your concentration, but it is the subconscious response which really does the work of bringing about the change within you. When you have learnt to develop concentration, you can move on to the all-important step of activating the great storehouse of the subconscious mind: the memory.

4

Tap Your Invaluable Storehouse of Memory

*

Probably more has been written about the subconscious mind than about either the conscious or superconscious aspects. Theories abound, from different schools of psychology, about what exactly this aspect of mind is and how it functions. To some extent it remains a mystery because of its very brilliance. It is a fantastic storehouse of mental information—including the faculty of memory.

THE SUBCONSCIOUS MIND

Contrary to the negative concepts of the subconscious mind that you find in some branches of psychiatry, which almost suggest that is an area filled exclusively with fears, suppressions and childhood hang-ups, this aspect of mind is outstanding to the point where even modern science has not really been able to analyse how it achieves its myriad functions. For example, as you are reading this book, how is it that you are absorbing the sentence that you read? You are memorising, second by second, the words that went before, and putting them together into a coherent form which the conscious mind can then cope with. This is short-term memory. You are also drawing on the subconscious mind for long-term memory in order to make sense of the points being made. You have remembered, for example, a vocabulary through which you can understand and consciously interpret the sentences you read.

What actually enables us to walk, talk, run, sing, dance or any other movement of the body? We can do these things only because the subconscious mind has such an intimate knowledge of all the functions of the neurological system that it can give the right instructions to the body. This defies the conscious mind of any scientist or even any computer yet invented. The simplest person has a subconscious mind which surpasses the most brilliant scientist—but stored at a level he is not consciously aware of.

Most of the time we take this aspect of mind for granted, until we come across those very sad cases of partial or complete memory loss which can make life seem almost unbearable. Even a bad case of forgetfulness can be a terrible burden to live with, and to some extent we have all suffered the limitations of an inability to remember someone or something. The main point to recognise is that you can do something about it. Memory can be improved and developed. The secret is to draw consciously on the subconscious mind and bring forth the information you require.

Through their analysis of brain cells, neuroscientists are beginning to make some headway on what memory is. They have found that when an animal is experiencing new sensations or entering new areas of life, specific cells in its central nervous system change their properties. These changes have been measured by watching electrical charges change as their membrane structures alter, and changes in blood flow and oxygen uptake have also been measured. Neurophysiologists watch the chemical transmitters that allow a signal to jump from one neuron to the next, out of millions of nerve cells in the brain. They hope to have some conclusive answers with the dawn of the twenty-first century.

MEMORISING FACTS

So how does the memory best respond to our conscious mind? If you wish to memorise something, it is best to go through it first and make sure you fully understand it. Of course, it is possible to learn things by rote, using one method or another of memorisation, but it is far more effective, especially in the long term, to have a full understanding of something if you wish to recall it later. For example, politicians who are able to remember facts and figures when they are under pressure to do so in debate are usually the ones who have a good grasp of the subject they are discussing. Whether their views are right or wrong is not necessarily relevant, although the sub-conscious mind will generally respond far better to truth than to falsehood. The important point is that there should be a coherent logic and an understanding in your own mind about the facts you are trying to remember.

Just reading about something does not necessarily mean you will remember it. You can read and re-read a book, but unless the subject has really captured your interest there is no guarantee that you will memorise the facts. Students who are studying for exams can come unstuck on this: they may spend hours revising the subject on which they will be tested, with the mistaken idea that this is really going to help them in their studies. You have to do far more than this if you want to be sure to store the information in your memory. You need to seek out the real meaning of what you are reading; you need to think about it and even come to your own opinions and feelings about it. What you feel about a subject can be far more crucial in helping you remember than your intellectual absorption of it—conviction and memory can work together. On the other hand, if you are too emotional about a subject, and therefore stressed about it, some blocking mechanisms may occur in the subconscious mind which prevent you from remembering it. The best frame of mind to be in is one of great interest and coherence, with a definite feeling about it— but no emotionalism.

In trying to memorise facts it can be very helpful to read them aloud rather than just think about them. This can provide a discipline for your mind, and the more the conscious mind focuses on the subject, the more likely it is to be stored in and recalled from your subconscious mind. It is amazing, as subliminal advertisers have discovered, just how much the subconscious mind registers. But if it is registered at a purely subliminal level—that is, without your consciously realising it—there is no guarantee that you will be able to recall the information when you need it. If you want this interrelationship between the conscious and the subconscious minds, which we call memory, then you need to register something deliberately, at a conscious level, in order to store it at a subconscious level and have it available on demand.

CONFIDENCE

Using the subconscious mind in this way requires great faith in its abilities, and there is plenty of evidence to justify this. You can rest assured that within you there is a tremendous storehouse of knowledge and information, most of which you are not consciously aware of at all. Realising this should give you greater confidence in your memory and your ability to draw on it as and when you wish.

Confidence will be reinforced by success. If you constantly say, 'I can't remember this or that,' you are reinforcing the idea that you do not have a good memory and that you do not have control over your subconscious mind. The fact is that you *can* remember, but you do not wish to exert the effort to do so at the time. It would be better to say not, 'I can't remember,' but just something like, 'It will come back to me later.' The next time you are in a conversation and something comes up which you do not remember, even though you have known about it in the past, discipline yourself to remember. You do not need to break off the conversation, but just put it on the shelf, as it were, and say to yourself, 'I'm going to remember this fact.' Then allow a gestation period to take place in the subconscious mind until it flashes through the conscious mind, which it will do if you place the necessary demand on it.

This can be very difficult at first, especially if you have had an undisciplined approach to memory in the past. Forgetfulness is really a form of mental laziness from which we all suffer to a greater or lesser extent. It should be regarded as such, rather than as something that is out of your control. As with all the powers of the mind, the first key is to have confidence in your own innate abilities, to realise the wonderful potential which lies within you in terms of mind power, and then gradually to release it. 'Realise—then release' is an excellent formula for expressing the magic of your mind.

MEMORY TECHNIQUES

Boredom is the worst enemy of memory. If there is something you have to remember, try to find some angle to it that interests you, even if it means mentally challenging some of the points you are trying to learn. Anything that stirs up a controversy in your mind will be more exciting and therefore easier to remember. Developing a real interest and fascination in something is the best way to remember it. Use your imagination and visualisation about a subject you are learning rather than just leaving it as intellectual concepts and words. For example, if you are learning about history, try to imagine the scenes you are learning about visually in your mind. If you do this you are far more likely to remember them later.

One particular technique which has been recommended for learning, especially for students, is to visualise in handwriting the words you have to remember. Rather than just reading, go through this process of mentally writing these words in your imagination and you may find later that you will be able to draw on them more easily. You can imagine them being written either in a book or on a blackboard in chalk. Do not attempt to do this to too many words at once and you will find that it is a way of learning some of the key words that you need to remember.

When learning something, it is much better to give your full concentration to it. For example, some people will have music or the television on and be reading at the same time. This causes a break in their concentration constantly from one source of material to another, even if they are not aware of it consciously, and this will lower their capacity to remember. A study of forty law students in the United States proved that they remembered information much better if they were not listening to music at the time.

Some people will use specific techniques of memory, such as catchphrases. For example, in England, the phrase 'Richard Of York Gave Battle In Vain' is used to remember the seven major colours of the rainbow in order: red-orange-yellow-green-blue-indigo-violet. Some people, when remembering names such as Brown Addison Lee and Downs, will take the first letter of each name to make the word 'bald'. These techniques can be very useful for passing exams and so on but are not a long-term way to improve your memory.

Researchers have found that physical exercise, as well as helping the body, helps the functions of the brain, and this applies to all aspects of mind. It is vital to stay mentally active if you wish to keep your memory sharp, particularly in the case of older people who may feel they are losing their mental powers. Often, when people retire, there is a danger that they may vegetate mentally by no longer participating in lively conversations or having the demands of concentration at a job. They may sink into television-watching and general inactivity. Retirement, however, is potentially one of the most productive periods of life, a time when you can study, explore and learn things that you have always wanted to; there is no need to lose your mental faculties to the degree that some people think. In a comparative study of people aged over 70, when compared with college students, Dr Morris Moscovitch of the University of Toronto found that the older people were less forgetful than the younger people. They were more conscientious and made notes more frequently as aids to memory.

As well as exercising the body and the mind, diet is always very important to all forms of mental health, including memory. A balanced intake of vitamins, minerals and amino acids is crucial. Elderly people with memory problems who have had a full physical examination and nutritional assessment, and who have acted on the advice given in terms of multivitamin and mineral supplements, have found improvement to their memories and mental faculties in general.

The memory functions in many different ways. Some psychologists refer to sensory memory as opposed to intellectual memory. If one of the physical senses is used to memorise something, it is far more effective than just relying on the intellect. Some say that hearing is more conducive to memory than seeing, although of course this will vary from person to person. For example, if you wish to remember something, it can be a good idea, rather than reading it to yourself, to read it aloud, record it on a tape and then listen back to it. This can lodge information more securely in your memory. When trying to remember people, it can be far easier to remember them from characteristics which have been conveyed to you emotionally or through the feelings, rather than relying purely on a physiological picture of their faces. When meeting someone for the first time, anything unusual that he tells you about himself will spark off a sympathetic trigger within you, which may be the key fact by which you remember him. If you have to remember people as part of your job or social life, this is a point well worth considering. When you meet a person, try to find some aspect of him that triggers a response in yourself, and then you may find it far easier to put a face to a name later on.

Another frequently used method of memorising is to use rhyme. If something is in rhyme it is far more interesting and therefore easier to recall than a straightforward statement of prose. For example, 'Thirty days have September, April, June and November' is easier to remember than 'There are thirty days in April, June, September and November'. Or 'In fourteen hundred and ninety-two, Columbus sailed the ocean blue' is easier to remember than 'Columbus sailed the ocean in fourteen hundred and ninety-two'.

However, these kinds of memory methods, while very useful for certain specific purposes, will not on their own deal with the long-term goal of improving your memory in general.

MEMORY IMPROVEMENT

You must always remember that your potential is perfection. It would of course be absurd actually to believe you are manifesting this perfection, but to say that you are perfect in potential gives you confidence about what you can become in the future. All effective methods of mental improvement rely on this type of mental confidence. Our natural state is one of perfection, and we ourselves have put up the obstacles which we now have to remove.

This is particularly true of memory and, providing it is done in a balanced and careful way, you can become far more effective in remembering all things—especially important ones—than you have been in the past. If you concern yourself too much with irrelevant data, however, you will not necessarily improve your memory in the right way. It is far better to use this faculty in a really useful way than to try memorise facts for the sake of them. The absentminded expert is someone who has managed to retain a massive amount of information about some obscure speciality which will not be useful or applicable in most areas of his life, yet he might regularly leave his house locked, with the key inside. He has developed his memory down a certain line but not in complete balance.

The most extreme cases of this can lead to a form of mental illness. Solomon Shereshevski could remember a random sequence of more than fifty numbers in less than three minutes. He could hold this memory for a matter of years and yet he had great difficulty in merging his perception of people. Because his memory was so acutely developed to an unusual degree, a face seen from the front and the side became two separate memories for him. He reached the point where he was unable to forget images and would confuse them with present perceptions. This, it must be said, is an extraordinary case, but it does bring us back to the basic guideline of not forcing our mind in any particular direction but rather allowing it to manifest its true potential. This approach can be slower than some memory techniques, but it will bring more solid and lasting benefits.

The two main qualities you need to develop an excellent memory are patience and determination. You need patience to avoid the temptation of always looking things up or asking other people what you have forgotten. Every time you do this you send a signal to your subconscious mind that you cannot remember and the memory will become more and more lazy. If, on the other hand, you patiently persist in trying to remember, the subconscious mind will get the message that you are going to do this and it will learn to co-operate. After all, the subconscious mind is there to help us function and, providing it is given the right signals, it will co-operate with us.

As well as this patient persistence, you will need determination to place that demand and remember something. This is not a determination which is strained or forced, but more a gentle resolution in the certain knowledge that you do have the fact you are trying to remember in your subconscious mind. Patience will oil the lock and determination will turn the key.

Below is an exercise which you can use to help improve your memory.

EXERCISE SEVEN: Memory Improvement

Sit, as in the previous exercises, in a calm but alert manner. Start to breathe rhythmically and without strain. Then make a point of remembering everything that happened yesterday morning. Go through the whole morning in your mind, item by item. If there is a blank spot and you are not sure what you did between, say, 11.00 and 11.30, determine to remember and sit patiently until you do.

This exercise will be very easy for some people and not so easy for others. For those who find it easy, make a very detailed recollection, even down to minute-by-minute events and changes. When exactly did you have that cup of coffee? When did you make that phone call to such and such a person? This will be especially powerful if you were doing something important which has an effect on you today and from which you need to take further action in the future. You will find your subconscious mind co-operates with you even more than if it was just some nondescript morning of little consequence.

If yesterday morning is too easy, then make it the week before or even earlier than that. The important point is that you do not give up. You go through the morning step by step, determined patiently to recall everything that you did. If you do this regularly, you will train your subconscious mind to co-operate with your conscious mind and you will find that you are able to recall things better throughout your life. It is one thing to try and remember something in the heat of the moment, and another to put aside some time gently to train your subconscious mind.

MEMORY TRAINING

Psychologists tell us that the subconscious mind tends to block unpleasant memories. This can be true and it may take some psychotherapy, or regression in certain cases, to bring to mind some of the events which a person has blocked off and refuses to remember. For example, those with very traumatic childhoods may block out their memories of what happened to them until it is brought out in consultation with a psychotherapist. There are many cases where psychotherapy has helped individuals to bring forth memories which were deeply buried, yet were distorting their behaviour at a subconscious level. On a more positive note, certain cultures, in teaching their history, have used the fact that we find it easier to remember happy and glorious events. They have gone out of their way to make the past as memorable as possible. The Greeks did this with their legends and the Vikings with their sagas. It is far easier to remember things when they are portrayed in a picturesque and heroic manner, combined with certain religious or moral overtones, than when they are just written up as dry, factual history.

During a lecture tour I made of New Zealand, I had the pleasure to meet a leading Tohunga, one of the elders of the Maoris. We were being driven to a television studio in Wellington by a Maori driver who was dumbfounded to find that the Tohunga could tell him the entire history of his family. Through elaborate carvings and other methods the Maori elders have developed the most phenomenal ability to remember historical and family details even down to the most minute detail. Although this Tohunga had never met the driver before, he could tell him much about his family history that was new to him.

If there is something particular that you need to remember, always try to make a firm mental impression of it on yourself. Do not just think about it once, but try to visualise what it is. For example, if you have a bunch of keys and you are told that the red key goes in one door, the blue in another and the yellow in a third, try actually to visualise the red key in one door, the blue key in the second and the yellow key in the third. This visualisation will feed your subconscious mind more fuel to enable you to bring this memory to mind when you need it.

Ultimately it is not a question of how good your memory is, because in potential everybody's memory can be good. It is how well you have been trained to use it. The information is all there, but have you developed the ability to tap it? A good memory is one of the most useful attributes you can have, especially in the modern world of facts, figures and data. Of course, you can use notes or files and should do so with important information. I am not suggesting that you take the risk of not recording vital pieces of information in order to train your memory. But when you do have the opportunity, instead of relying on notes or other people, insist that your own subconscious mind gives you the information you need.

Use the tools of enthusiasm, excitement and even passion to help you remember things. If you read a novel with great feeling, you are far more likely to remember the details later. Try to have confidence in the subject you are dealing with, since it is much easier to remember something you know you are good at. In this sense it is rather like a virtuous circle: your confidence in your ability to remember details about a particular subject will feed your ability to do so and your memory will be like an upward spiral, getting better and better. On the other hand, if you feel that you will never be able to remember anything about it, this lack of confidence will tend to reinforce your disability.

If you have a developed intuition you will find that how you programme yourself to remember is critically important, for that is virtually what you are doing when you try to memorise something. If you are given some information about a person which you intuitively feel is incorrect but nevertheless you receive it and try to store it in your memory bank, you may have more difficulty remembering it later. It would be better in that case to note your intuitive feelings and reprogramme yourself together with your own feelings about the subject. Then you have made a self-programme about something which is true to your own feelings, and there will not be any conflicting thoughts to block your memory.

For example, you may find that you do not really believe in the version of an event reported in a newspaper. You have a gut feeling that it is biased in some way, perhaps politically. You do not, however, consciously register these reservations, you just have a strange feeling about it. If, instead, you allowed your intuition to speak to you and thought consciously, 'Well, I don't really believe the bias which is being put on this story, I'm not even sure whether it is true; but that is what the newspaper says,' then you would find it much easier to remember the report later on.

It is easy to prove how important motivation is to memory. If somebody came up to you and told you that if you remembered a certain sentence you would win £1,000, you would find it very easy to remember. If the person just told you that he would be grateful if you would remember it, you would be far less likely to do so. The motivation of a financial reward would make all the difference, but it also proves that you can remember something if you are sufficiently motivated to do so. You must therefore cultivate this motivation.

REINCARNATION

It would be remiss to include a chapter on improving your memory without referring to reincarnation. There are those, including myself, who believe that we have lived many past lives and that the memory of these past lives is locked up within us, mainly to help us and to avoid confusion. If you do not believe in reincarnation, you will have no chance of recalling your previous lives because they will be locked within you and that blockage will be reinforced by the programme you have given your subconscious mind, that this is the only life you have ever led. Certain feelings and vague thoughts may emerge; you may have some kind of knowledge about a place, a person, or a subject which you have not learnt in this life, but you will not know why. Some people have been hypnotically regressed into their previous lives and have revealed detailed memories while in a hypnotic trance of events and places which they could not have consciously known, thereby proving to the sceptic a very strong case for reincarnation. But this is not the best way to remember past lives. It would be far better if you could gradually, gently, awaken the memories yourself as and when they became useful to you.

Some people are so fascinated by medieval tournaments that they spend their weekends dressing up as knights and jousting. Why? Others get a tremendous thrill from 'reliving' the battles of Waterloo or the American Civil War in full costume. Why? There are those who are obsessed from child-hood with a particular Eastern religion, even though they have no experience of it in this life. These and many other examples abound to support the case for reincarnation. Past life memory requires advanced yoga techniques and should be done carefully, with a great deal of discrimination.

Whether you subscribe to the theory of reincarnation or not, you will find that a determined effort to improve your memory will unlock the door to a storehouse of knowledge and infor-mation which is not only extremely valuable to you, but can help you greatly in any endeavour you are engaged upon. In reality we never forget anything, it is only a question of learn-ing to remember.

5

The Benefits of Creative Visualisation

*

As well as mastering the essential skills of concentration and memory which are primarily associated with the left hemisphere of the brain, it is equally important to develop the creative aspect of your consciousness, which is associated with the right-hand side. To do this you need to activate the faculty of imagination which was very well summed up by Dr George King as being man's only creative faculty. This simple but true statement clearly expresses the vital importance of developing and using this creative power in your life.

IMAGINATION

Imagination can be used in virtually every area of life, from the most mundane activity to the most far-reaching. The same faculty which is used to plan a family outing is also used in other circumstances to manifest the genius of our inspired poets, artists and composers. It is imagination which leads the scientist beyond the known laws into the realms of real scientific advancement. Without imagination we would all be dull, repetitive, robot-like people who never expanded our horizons into new areas of achievement. You could say that the hallmark of real human achievement is the applied use of imagination.

We are all imagining things all the time. For example, how often do we fantasise about being promoted at work, having greater wealth than we have at present, or going out with a particular man or woman of our choice? On a more important level, how often do we think of world peace dawning on Earth, of an end to violence in a particular region such as the Middle East? How often do we think of poverty and starvation coming to an end? Some would say that thoughts such as these are mere daydreaming, escapism from the everyday realities of life. In one way this may be true, but in another way, when we think of such positive imaginings we are creating a positive thought form which will affect us and our approach to life.

Some of those who teach meditation techniques stress this as the main benefit of such practices. They say that so powerful are the thoughts transmitted in meditation or deep contemplation that these thoughts, elevated as they are, must have some effect on the world as a whole and, in some cases, a very definite effect. In our imaginings, we are creating thought patterns which will radically change ourselves and, to a greater or lesser extent, others too.

Of course the imaginings and fantasies of most people are very heavily influenced by current fashions, media trends and the influences of the environment in which they find themselves. Being subjected to constant images through advertising and popular culture in general greatly affects our immediate thinking processes. We find ourselves imagining scenes which have been conjured up visually or verbally for us. Advertising is based on the premise that our dreams will be fulfilled. Advertisers will portray a certain product as being glamorous and associated with beautiful men or women, luxury and other tempting images. They know that many of those watching will later imagine themselves in these situations and will go out and buy the product on the basis that it will open doors for them. Often this is not true and the advertisements are therefore using misinformation to fire up the imagination of those who would not otherwise buy their products. The morality of this is a question for debate, but whether you think it is a good or bad thing, it certainly does prove the power of imagination. After all, if the viewer of a particularly attractive advertisement did not imagine herself in that situation, then the advertisement would not work. Very often these imaginings take place at an almost instinctive level: the person does not think about them consciously but finds fleeting images passing through her mind—images which lead to subconscious associations.

VISUALISATION EXERCISES

In order to manifest your inner potential you need to use your imagination actively and deliberately, through creative visualisation. You need to monitor where your thoughts and fantasies and daydreams lead you and try to bring them under direct control. After all, the whole essence of using mind power is to control it, virtually to have it available to your disposal. That is why creative visualisation is so very important. In a visualisation exercise you are choosing the thing you wish to happen, knowing that it will have a definite and direct effect on your future thinking process and thereby on your life as a whole.

So many visualisations that people have are negative. They do not realise that a negative visualisation will affect them and possibly others, and so they allow their minds to wander over negative happenings. Of course, it is very important to be familiar with the news, which unfortunately is predominantly bad—at least according to the media reports we receive. There is a strong argument for introducing more positive news into these reports in order to give food for people's positive approach. But even though we need to know about forest fires, earthquakes, poverty, starvation, wars and so forth, we do not need to dwell on the negativity associated with these events. If we do dwell on them, then we are giving mental power to those events.

This principle is regarded by practitioners of all forms of magic as the key to success: whatever you dwell on you also give power to. It would be far more useful to read the news or see it on television, accept it as being fact but frame your imagination along positive lines, such as the positive things that could happen in those areas and the good that could come out of them. Those who pray for world peace are doing just this in a most definite and direct manner. They are sending out positive thoughts to the world, depending of course on the potency and wording of the prayers. With prayer, visualisation is doubly important because a spiritual invocation is being made which gives tremendous power to the mental visualisation. For example, if you are praying for a war-torn area, it is much better not only to send out a positive beam of mental thought—to pray for healing and peace and well-being—but actually to visualise these things happening. If in your prayer you visualise the suffering, the calamity and all the negative things surrounding the area for which you are praying, then you may give power to them, which is the exact opposite of what you are trying to achieve.

When exercising the power of the mind through creative visualisation, one of the first things you start to realise is that you are dealing with a scientific procedure. It is not a question of your intention or your motive. Although good intentions and good motives are valuable, even essential, they are not good enough to guarantee the result. In fact, there is great truth in the old adage: 'The road to hell is paved with good intentions'! Success is determined by the degree of positive visualisation you put behind whatever act in which you are engaged.

This applies not only to specific exercises and practices, but also throughout your life. You will find that if you set aside some time every day to perform exercises, they will have an effect on the whole of your life. In other words, you do not just do a practice for the benefit it brings you in the ten or fifteen minutes that it lasts, you do it for the benefit it will bring you in everything you do, both waking and sleeping. You will find that a positive visualisation can stay with you for some time and, if it becomes regular, will start to affect all your thoughts for the better. It will start to permeate your thinking process rather in the same way that a beneficial programme of vitamin and mineral supplements will permeate your physical structure. I recommend that you repeat the same visualisation frequently until you have attained success with it, and after that as often as necessary.

CONTROLLING IMAGINATION

Thoughts enter the brain in habitual patterns. If you continue to expose yourself to a certain type of literature, conversation or company, then you will end up behaving and thinking in that way. For example, those of you who have children know that the sort of company they keep will affect not only their behaviour but also their language, their dress, their music, their approach to work, their manners and many other aspects of their lives. That is why some parents are so worried about their children falling into bad company: they fear the influence of their companions as well as the familiarity with their types of thought and cultural behaviour patterns. The youngsters start thinking in the same way and, even though their true nature may be different, habitual thought patterns emerge, causing their mode of behaviour to change.

This tendency can be turned to advantage. Those who study uplifting spiritual or philosophical literature, who frequent places where spiritual patterns of behaviour are being followed, where service is being performed with a heart full of love for others, will also start to become changed in their mental processes by the thought patterns to which they are exposing themselves.

This underlines the vital need to gain control over the power of your imagination. Even though you may have to mix in company you would really rather not, or may have to expose yourself to sad or unpleasant environments, your imagination will be the key force. But there is a word of warning for those who have to deal with the negative behaviour patterns of others: always protect yourself by constantly refreshing your mind with positive visualisation. How many policemen who have gone undercover to perform brave and heroic work have been tarnished by the company they have been forced to mix with? A minority certainly, but nevertheless a small number who, tragically, when exposed to the temptations of wealth and apparent comfort enjoyed by the criminal fraternity, turn and leave the noble path upon which they had set their course. When I say apparent comfort, of course, it is only a materialistic comfort and since feeling comfortable is a state of mind, those with a developed conscience cannot really enjoy it.

Some of those on the path of yoga went out of their way to put themselves in painful situations, states of privation and near starvation in order to demonstrate the power of the mind. They maintained and demonstrated that it was possible to be in a state of peace and bliss despite all material conditions. I am certainly not advocating that the average person needs to attempt to do this, but it is a lesson to us all. It does show that the visualisation of your mind determines your state of being far more than the material conditions of life. How many millionaires are unsatisfied because they wish they were multimillionaires? There is no end to the desire for material gain and there is no point at which you can say you are fully satisfied. If you use your mind you can achieve satisfaction through the correct use of the imagination and other techniques which I shall cover later in this book. If you learn to do these things regularly, you will find that gradually you will be able, at a time of your own choosing, to bring about the mental state you wish to achieve. This will not happen overnight, but it is a goal to strive for.

The key to developing the power of your imagination is practice. All too often we are embroiled in a very busy life and are not necessarily able to enjoy the balance we need. To find true balance we need all the elements—air, fire, earth, water and the mysterious fifth element of ether—to be present and in harmony. According to ancient mystic writings, these elements contain more than their physical aspect, they also have an effect on the natural universal energies of mind and draw to us those mental essences that we need. If we are lacking in any particular one, it is advantageous to focus our visualisation upon that particular element in order to attract the vital energies it brings. The following visualisation practice has been carefully conceived to include all the elements so that if any one particular element is not in balance in your life at any particular time, it will be sure to come to you through this exercise, provided you use your imagination in an active and controlled manner as fully as you possibly can.

EXERCISE EIGHT:
Creative Visualisation Using the Elements

As in previous exercises, start by sitting in your usual position and breathe deeply and rhythmically for a few minutes. Then transport yourself, mentally, to a country location of your own choosing. This can either be a place that you know or an imaginary place which you particularly like. For example, if you are attracted to rolling countryside, that will be fine. Alternatively, you may be someone who likes the thrill of mountaineering or a large and beautiful garden set around a lake. Choose your scene carefully and make sure that the weather conditions there are very clement, neither too hot nor too cold.

The sun should be shining upon you and you feel its rays upon your skin. Try to feel the warmth which is associated with being in the sun, even though you may be indoors when you do this practice. *This is the element of fire.*

You are standing on the earth and you should feel the earth beneath your feet. It may be the green grass of a field or the ledge of a cliff, but if it is the ledge of a cliff, it must be safe. There are no other human beings around you, you are completely alone, but you have contact with the ground and *this is the element of earth.*

There is a light breeze, not a hurricane or a heavy wind, just a light, gentle breeze wafting past you and you feel this as it wafts and slightly ruffles your skin and hair as it does so. *This is the element of air.*

Not far from you there is water. For example, there may be a river or a stream gently, not ferociously, running past you. You can hear the ripple of the water, you can dip your hand into the water and feel its coolness. If you are on a mountain, it should have a little lake upon it or near it. You can walk to this water and dip your hand in it and feel the cool, pleasant liquid as you do so. Perhaps you like to put your hands against your face, in your imagination, and feel the cold water pleasantly against your skin. *This is the element of water.*

All around you is the beautiful sensation of nature's beauty, and the natural living energies which come from nature revive all those who have the good sense to spend some time alone in a natural environment. You can start to feel this uplifting energy coursing through you. This represents *the element of ether*, which includes and extends beyond all the other elements.

This exercise should be done carefully and with great control. You may not be able to spend very long on any one element, but you must incorporate all of them. You may find that a particular element will get a little out of control—the wind may start to get too strong, or the water may begin to churn up; you may feel the earth beneath you not as firm as it should be, or you may be a little burnt by the sun. If any of these things start to happen, control your imagination and bring your visualisation back to the original starting point. In other words, don't allow any of these elements to get out of control. Keep the water very calm, the breeze very light, the sun warm but not too hot and the earth firm beneath your feet. Above all, the mysterious element of ether will come to you, reviving you, restoring your spirits and preparing you for the travails of everyday life.

If for any reason you find that you are not able to do this visualisation and that it does get out of control, then leave it for a while and practise more simple affirmations and exercises before trying it again. But when you do, you must make sure that you succeed because this will have a very definite effect upon your life and, providing it is controlled, will be very beneficial. It will not be the same as physically going to the environment you visualised, although it can have some positive physical effects, but on a mental level it will certainly be extremely good for you and will give you the energy and the power you need to go about your daily life fortified by the balanced input of energy from all five elements.

Good luck with this practice. Do it correctly and it will enhance your life in ways that will pleasantly surprise you. Done regularly and with enough concentration, it will bring balance into your life wherever it was lacking. You should not do it every day, but certainly it can be done every week or less frequently—whenever you feel the need for it. It is an exercise for charging you up emotionally as well as mentally, and will be very effective at times when you feel life has become mundane and meaningless. It will tend to invigorate you and draw inspiration to you, as well as bringing back a certain *joie de vivre*. You should develop a love for it and look forward to practising it—but use it sparingly. Every time you do it, give it your all—then you will get the best out of it and it will not lose its power through overfamiliarity. In this sense, it is rather like a special treat: If you had it too often it would no longer be special and would therefore lose its thrill. Unlike some of the previous exercises, which can be done daily or very regularly, keep this one for those occasions when you are really in the mood, and it will develop a powerful magic for good in your life.

6

Enhancing Your Personality

*

Mind is expressed through individuality. Just as you can gain control over your mental abilities, such as concentration, memory and imagination, so you can control your individual expression through personality. You can change and mould your personality naturally, within the parameters of your innate characteristics, but this needs to be done carefully to bring out the best in you.

If you are entirely satisfied with your personality, then there is something wrong with it! An honest self-examination by any one of us would reveal areas where we were lacking and where we needed to improve.

On the other hand, it would be equally unbalanced to dislike yourself or regard yourself as irretrievably flawed. We need to learn to love ourselves as well as others in order to enhance and improve our personalities. After all, if we have no love for ourselves then we shall have no concern whether or not we amount to anything.

SELF-KNOWLEDGE

The key to enhancing personality and personal magnetism is, as the ancient Greeks said, to 'know thyself, and you will know the Gods and their energies'. There is nothing sadder than a person who has completely the wrong self-image. He believes that he's a certain type of person when in fact he is not, so he is constantly disappointed. It is important to know your own mind, for a certain wisdom comes with self-knowledge. You can always recognise the person who knows his own shortcomings and yet has a very good idea of his strengths also; in fact, personal strength goes hand-in-hand with personal self-knowledge, providing you remain positive about life. You do not want the kind of self-knowledge that makes you become too negative about yourself and develop a failure complex. On the contrary, the key to enhancing your personality is to know and feel right about who you are; only then will you have a firm foundation on which to build.

There are certain specific attributes you can develop that will enhance your personality. These vary from person to person, and if you practise self-examination you will be able to see where improvement is required. For example, if you are an extremely indecisive person, you may wish to focus on becoming more decisive. If you are very short-tempered you will wish to focus on becoming more patient, and so on. Just by accepting the challenge of your failings and determining to do something about them, you have already turned the corner. You have made a positive determination and you honestly believe that you can change your weaknesses and enhance your strengths. You do need to find your own way of doing this, since what works for one will not necessarily work for another. It is no good trying to be something you are not.

For example, if you are a naturally humorous person and this is one of your strengths, you can use it to overcome certain weaknesses. Let us say you are a humorous person who has a very bad temper and you wish to maintain your cheerful sense of humour but control your bad temper. Use your humour when next you lose your temper; use your positive attribute to overcome the negative one. When you feel extremely bad-tempered, try to see the funny side of it, which you are already good at doing, and this will be a key in developing the patience you also need.

To take another example, you might be a very lethargic person but you do have a wide variety of interests. You can use the positive attribute of having a wide variety of interests to overcome your lethargy. Apply yourself to your interests when you next feel lethargic, instead of leaving them as only theory. In each case the discipline and effort involved will allow your personality to come through by using an attribute of your own.

ENTHUSIASM

One trait which always comes through any positive personality is enthusiasm. If you meet an enthusiastic person, someone who really is happy to meet you, she has a very decided impact on you. If you meet someone who really could not care less, then you very often could not care less either. Personality interchange is reciprocal—what you give out you get back. Enthusiasm is the carrier wave to project your personality, and if you have enthusiasm for what you are doing, you will put your all into it and will be far more likely to succeed. If you are enthusiastic about your job, your religion, your family or whatever else you may be involved in, that enthusiasm will carry you through to success. So this is something we all need to develop if we wish to have a positive personality.

Of course the way we express this enthusiasm can be very different and depends on our own individual set of characteristics, but the enthusiasm will be the same force manifesting in different ways in different people.

The next time you have to go to a social function that you do not really wish to attend, discipline yourself to go with enthusiasm. Make a point of projecting this enthusiasm to all whom you meet, and leave when the function ends having really put your all into it. The next time you are required to do a job which you find tedious, go out of your way to find something about it which really interests you. When you find this, pursue it with enthusiasm. There must be some aspect to everything which has a positive focus for you. Either somebody is benefiting and that is enough to fire your enthusiasm, or you will learn something through doing the job which you have never learnt before—maybe you will meet somebody new or go somewhere new. There is always an aspect which you can find to cultivate your enthusiasm. This is not easy, particularly if it is something you have become accustomed to dreading, perhaps over several years. But if you attack the project and determine to meet it with enthusiasm, you will find that this is an attribute which soon becomes available to you virtually 'on tap'. This one characteristic of enthusiasm can enhance your personality immensely.

Yogis who found a weakness in their nature would sometimes go out of their way to expose themselves to it so that they could overcome it. They would find, for example, a pursuit which they considered to be particularly dull and make a point of searching out something interesting in it. Many yoga practices are extremely repetitive and, on the face of it, very boring. It is only the interchanges going on within you that make them interesting. The same can be true of any pastime. For example, if you loathe ironing or washing up or some other mundane task, make a point of doing it and finding something rewarding about it. After all, at the end of the day, these activities produce beneficial results. It is really a question of how you look at things. You can change your approach instantaneously if you decide to, and the more you get used to doing this, the more you will be able to do it. Never be governed by the materialistic environment in which you live.

You may have found that when you are irritable, tired, nervous or anxious, annoyance from the neighbours can be extremely upsetting. But if you are happy and contented, the same noise doesn't bother you at all. It is not the noise which has changed, it is your state of mind, and this, cultivated within you at will, can enhance your personality immeasurably.

As with enthusiasm, so with joy. Some people believe that happiness is something they either have or do not have. They believe it is beyond their control and that if they are happy they are lucky, while if they are unhappy it is just their unfortunate lot. Those who believe in a law of Karma governing all action believe that we get what we deserve anyway—what goes around comes around. But you can still find yourself falling into that trap of feeling miserable and thinking it is somebody else's fault. Again, happiness and misery are states of mind which can be cultivated or avoided. Some mystics used to go out of their way deliberately to develop joy. They would pick any pursuit and perform it with as much joy as they possibly could.

Of course there are events in our lives which would cause grief to any of us and we have to be realistic about this. You should never repress your true feelings, only learn to control them. We all know those people who are constantly miserable, moaning and groaning and making themselves and everybody else feel worse. They do not even have to open their mouths to bring down the atmosphere in a room. If you have a tendency to be miserable, go out of your way to develop joy. Look at things in a different light, try to find something positive about everything around you—it is always there if you only look for it. This will greatly enhance your personality. If you are a happy and enthusiastic person, whether you be extroverted or introverted, inclined to physical or mental pursuits, the inherent qualities of enthusiasm and joy will shine through your personality like a radiant light, enhancing your whole character. We are not born with unalterable personalities which are beyond our control, like some baggage which is tied to our backs. We can select the personality traits that we wish to enhance and those that we wish to remove. It is all a question of effort, determination and a positive approach.

OVERCOMING WEAKNESSES

If you have a specific weakness you wish to overcome, you can always devise a suitable positive suggestion, as described in Chapter Three. Dr Shastri taught two possible wordings which can be used in affirmations. The first is to start a sentence with the phrase, 'I hereby resolve to overcome . . .' and then to state what it is that you wish to overcome. For example, if you are always late for appointments, you would say, 'I hereby resolve to overcome my lack of punctuality.' Or to put it in a more positive way, you could say, 'I hereby resolve to become a punctual person.' You can say this to yourself either silently or out loud if you are alone. You will find that you gradually instruct yourself to do so. The other wording that Dr Shastri taught was, 'I command my mind to banish . . .' If there is a persistent thought or behaviour pattern that is troubling you, which you really do not wish to have, you can gain mastery over your mind and banish it from your thoughts. For example, if you are constantly thinking of overeating a particular type of food which is not good for you, you could say, 'I hereby resolve to banish my desire for such and such a food.' Both of these methods, according to Dr Shastri, work very well indeed.

It is well proven that hypnosis can help people to overcome habits such as smoking and it may be medically necessary for people to use this sort of treatment which is now medically approved. But it is far better from the point of view of your inner will-power to gain control over your own life using an affirmation. In a sense you are then performing positive self-hypnosis by instructing your subconscious mind how to behave, rather than being entranced by a hypnotist and receiving suggestions from an outside source.

If there is a particular habit you are trying to give up, invent an affirmation for it. Make it a positive one, but do be careful with the wording. You must never say, 'I have overcome such and such a thing.' You must always say, 'I resolve to overcome such and such a thing.' In other words, you must never lie to yourself because this will cause internal mental confusion. You must make it a positive determination for the future and always make it a realistic one. An affirmation must be about what you are going to do, not about what you have done.

The other great advantage of affirmation is that it develops your inherent self-confidence. Balanced confidence without egoism is another definite way of enhancing your personal magnetism.

I must stress that, when dealing with weaknesses, it is no solution to try to suppress them or push them under the surface. You have to resolve to change, but at the same time recognise the truth of your nature—and there is a very narrow dividing line here. Some criminals have argued that they are honest people because they have openly displayed the depravity of their nature. This is not honesty, it is weakness. They have not been true to their real selves which, though they may be deeply buried, do exist. They have only been true to certain wicked desires they have felt. Even some children have been filled with wicked desires and have carried out foul acts. Psychiatrists may tell us that it is all a result of mental illness, but while that is obviously true, it can also be used to undermine the need for personal responsibility or, if you like, personal choice. We can choose those personality traits we wish to enhance and those we wish to control. We cannot just shove them under the carpet and hope they will go away. We have to face up to what is there and then gradually try to change it by focusing on the positive. We should never be the slaves of mental impulses but always the controller.

ENHANCING SELF-IMAGE

You can enhance your self-image by bringing out those characteristics and urges within you that you know to be good and beneficial. It is not really complicated to work out which are positive and which are not. Those which are constructive, benign, helpful to others and yourself in all ways are the ones to develop. Those which are destructive and harmful to others are the ones which have to be controlled. We can all realise that we have within us the mental attributes necessary to enhance our personalities in the direction we choose. Focus always on the positive. Generate the sort of energy you want to radiate to others. Enthusiasm, joy, compassion, patience—you do not have to be a religious zealot to know that these qualities enhance any personality and that these and others like them are the qualities we should go out of our way to cultivate. When you appreciate the power of your mind, you start to realise that you can do something about your personality. It is not just something you were born with, over which you have no control. You can focus your mind on those aspects you wish to expand and detach your mind from those you want to starve virtually into non-existence—without trying to pretend that they are not there.

Enhancing personality and personal magnetism is not a selfish pursuit. On the contrary, it is a measure of your concern for others that you wish to do this. But you will get great pleasure from it, for the human psyche is happy when it is working properly. In that sense it is like a machine which, when it is operating as it was intended to do, radiates a certain energy which is akin to happiness. It is the same with all of us when we are functioning correctly. When you find out who you are, you are not deluding yourself that you are somebody else and you set out to enhance and improve yourself using positive affirmations, careful, honest self-examination and some of the other exercises in this book, you will find that you will unlock the power of your mind beyond your wildest imaginings.

None of us is stagnant or fixed. We are all in a constant state of change, and we can turn this change to our advantage by enhancing the positive attributes within us that we call our personality. You will have to be persistent in this quest for self-improvement. Do not be put off by mistakes or failings. Continue to seek mastery of the amazing potential within you and remember that sometimes it is not so much a question of being right, as being left. Pace yourself like a long distance runner and, despite any shortcomings along the way, you will find the goal you seek. The following is a simple but powerful exercise you can use to enhance your self-image.

EXERCISE NINE: Enhancing Your Self-Image

Sit comfortably with your eyes closed and practise harmonious breathing. To do this exercise properly you will need to develop a degree of self-knowledge. Start by reflecting upon one of your weaknesses, but without dwelling on it in a negative fashion. Just identify it and acknowledge that it exists. Then make an inner resolution to change it—your degree of commitment behind this resolution will determine the success of the exercise. Now visualise yourself changing in that respect. Go back to a situation where you exhibited this weakness and imagine yourself exhibiting a positive characteristic in its stead. If there are other people involved, do not imagine them changing at all, in fact try to concentrate on your own pattern of behaviour to the exclusion of all others. You should never try to use visualisation to control the behaviour of others—only your own.

By visualising this changed behaviour, you are correcting your self-image. You are seeing yourself in a new light, which feeds your subconscious mind with different signals about yourself. If you thought you were unkind, you will start to see yourself as kind and this visualisation will reflect upon your future behaviour—you will start to become more kind.

The second part of the exercise is an essential balance. Think of a good quality in your nature and resolve to enhance it. Think of a situation where you exhibited this good quality and resolve to manifest it through your personality more frequently.

This exercise will only be successful if you are entirely honest with yourself and very positive in your resolutions. It will then bring a marked change for the good to your life. It will help you to know yourself better and remove any confusion you may have felt about yourself. It will also make you a more understanding person with others as well as yourself. You will find that you develop more patience and strike a better balance in your approach by understanding but not condoning others' weaknesses. It should also make you less judgemental of others, because a person who knows herself is more tolerant generally. Having the right self-image is vital—how sad it is to meet those who really believe they are something they are not. This exercise will give you a better perspective on yourself, while at the same time giving power to your positive qualities and therefore enhancing those in your life.

You will find after doing the exercise for some time that you naturally project your positive qualities more easily. Do not practise it too often, since you do not want to overdo introspection and become self-centred, but you can certainly practise it on a weekly basis or less frequently than that. After doing the exercise several times you will become more self-assured and will radiate to others a greater degree of self-confidence than before. This will not be a surface extroversion but a deep confidence based upon self-knowledge.

PART TWO

DISCOVERING
SUPERMIND

7

Mind Over Matter

*

You have now mastered the essential faculties of mind that we all need for successful living. You have learnt how to bring your thoughts under control and direct them through concentration, memory and imagination into whatever channel you choose. You have discovered the secret of enhancing your personality—again in whatever direction you choose—knowing that your personality is not something unalterable with which you were endowed through genetics alone, but something you can change and develop at will.

So is that all there is to the journey into the realms of mind? No—thank goodness! That is just the beginning. Mind can tell us far more about life and the purpose of our real selves— not just our personalities, but our real selves. It can show us the massive human potential which is just waiting to be tapped and provide us with a deeper level of awareness than we thought possible. But to do this we have to leave the world of physics and enter the world of metaphysics or that which is beyond the physical. Purely material explanations cannot help us here, we have to examine the so-called paranormal sciences. It is no longer enough just to see mind as a product of the brain—as we journey into supermind we realise that it is something far more.

UNIVERSAL MIND

So where exactly is your mind? Metaphysical thinkers have concluded that mind is something universal, beyond the individual but which we have the facility, through the use of the brain, of tuning into. Only this concept explains fully the way our consciousness works.

Certainly, the brain is a wonderful thing. The very existence of such a brilliant mechanism, which cannot be duplicated by the most advanced computer technology, proves the wonder of human anatomy. Some would go farther and say it proves the existence of God. They would question how it could develop haphazardly without some divine force behind it. Others try to explain this marvellous human organism by an extension of Darwinism. They claim that in the same way as animals evolved through a process of natural selection, so the brain has developed the ability to generate extraordinary, complex linkages of the neurons that lie between our ears.

While these ideas are fascinating, they do not explain, for example, telepathy, which can take place between two minds. How many times have you thought and heard someone in the same room as you utter exactly the same words that you had just thought? How is it that trends and fashions develop in different parts of the world at the same time? Can it all be put down to the media and advertising, or could it be that a universal mind belt is being permeated with a certain type of thought form? Why is it that vastly different cultural regions decide to adopt communism or fascism, or some other form of political movement, at the same time in history? Could it be that the mind belt is being impressed with communistic thought forms and that these are being picked up all over the world by millions of people at the same time?

And if you go farther, how is it that clairvoyants are able accurately to tune in to events which have already happened but which they were not aware of, or indeed in some cases, events which have yet to happen? Metaphysicians say that these things are impressed so firmly in universal mind that the clairvoyant is able to tune in to it and interpret it.

DEMONSTRATIONS OF MIND POWER

There have been outstanding demonstrations of mind over matter. Practitioners of yoga have exhibited the ability to stop their hearts beating for extended periods, and yet have remained conscious and alive. Reports throughout history tell of cases where remarkable individuals have been known to disappear. One such was Apollonius of Tyana who lived in Greece in the first century AD. His outspoken criticisms of the Roman Emperor Domitian led to his captivity. He had already demonstrated remarkable powers of mind and had claimed to visit enlightened masters in India. Because Apollonius had been declared guilty of treason he was brought before Domitian himself, as was the custom, and according to legend he berated Domitian for his misuse of power over others. Then, just before the Emperor could sentence him to death, he disappeared. Reports have it that he was seen some time later in Greece teaching and, in front of a public audience, declared that he was witnessing the end of the 'tyrant'. It was later found, when the news reached that area, that this was the exact moment of the Emperor's death.

Stories like these abound and many attempt to debunk them. Indeed, there are some who make a living out of claiming that they can duplicate feats of mind over matter using conjuring tricks. Such an idea is absurd in my opinion. Of course conjurors can use their trickery to mislead a public audience, but this does not in any way undervalue or disprove the numerous demonstrations of mind over matter through history.

It is strange that, despite the many changes in physics and science in general, there always remains a hard core of people who seem intent on debunking the paranormal. It seems as though the very existence of paranormal phenomena is a threat to them. Hearteningly, there is an increasing number of scientists who take the opposite view. Research is going on into many aspects of so-called paranormal events which at one time would have been dismissed by the scientific community as preposterous. It is worth noting that Alexander Bell, who invented the telephone, was initially dismissed by the scientific community in Paris as a ventriloquist!

One phenomenon which was completely repudiated by orthodox scientists until recently is levitation—the ability to make objects float in mid-air. Some scientists in America now believe that this is possible. They say that the weight of objects can be altered using force fields. Since the 1940s scientists have known that the whole of space is filled with a sea of subatomic particles popping in and out of existence so fast that they cannot be seen. These are called vacuum fluctuations and have been measured in laboratories. It is now thought that these vacuum fluctuations produce a magnetic force which causes movement in the subatomic particles, and this itself is responsible for inertia. If these forces can be altered, then there could be some control over the movements of these objects—in other words levitation.

This is an exact explanation of metaphysical and mystical concepts propounded through the ages in East and West, except that there is one missing ingredient—universal mind. It is mind controlling these forces, which causes their interaction with the subatomic particles and the movement of the objects.

Many studies have been made of teleportation (the movement of objects through mind control), psychokinesis (the movement of physical objects through psychic powers) and other demonstrations of mind over matter. Some cynics use the so-called law of parsimony—that is, that one's own reason and physical laws should always be preferred over the more unusual esoteric theories—but there have been notable examples throughout history of scientists and philosophers who have taken a more truly open-minded approach. One was Sir Francis Bacon who, as well as being one of the finest intellects of the Elizabethan and Jacobean eras, and some would say the author of the greatest of Shakespeare's works, was a pioneering scientist. In his collection of essays, *Sylva Sylvarum: or a Natural History*, he postulated one of the most important approaches to scientific principles. His ideas on inductive reasoning and the experimental method, as it became known, can be summarised very simply. He said that instead of working on the basis of theories and then attempting to apply those theories to life, it would be far more profitable to observe life and then form conclusions. Although that sounds extremely obvious, it is invaluable to the understanding of the mind. So often scientists will tell you, based on their researches, what should happen, and therefore rule some metaphysical concepts of mind as impossible simply because they don't comply with their theories. Instead of this, it would be far more valuable to observe demonstrations and then form conclusions.

Let us take Uri Geller as an example. He has been vilified by many and it could be argued that he has attempted to turn his demonstrations of mind power into a show business circus. In my view, this is not the most valid way to use mind power, and I would also apply this to others who have demonstrated their abilities for wealth and fame. Of course they would counter this by saying that their real aim was to show people what can be achieved by mind over matter. But whatever the motive of the demonstrator, and the rights and the wrongs of this use of mind power, we are left at the end of the day with a demonstration. There is no doubt that in Uri Geller's first demonstrations in England in the early 1970s, many people claimed that knives, forks, spoons, keys and nails were bending in homes all over the country. This did not fit in with the scientific theories of many orthodox thinkers and so they attempted to debunk these demonstrations or to find some alternative explanation. If they had followed Sir Francis Bacon's great thesis that instead of trying to deduce life from theory, we should deduce theory from life, they would not have done this. Instead they would have attempted to discover what exactly was going on in these demonstrations and looked at them with a completely open mind.

Whatever your view of them, Uri Geller's demonstrations are by no means unique in history. Marc Thury, a professor of natural history and astronomy at the Academy of Geneva in the nineteenth century, performed experiments into telekinetic phenomena. He published a book in 1855 posing a theory which at that time was extremely controversial—that the unconscious mind could let loose psychic energies. He gave the example of an 11-year-old boy who had been practising psychokinesis. According to Thury, objects were moving in response to his unconscious desires or thoughts. For example, his music lessons were repeatedly interrupted by the levitation of his piano, although others would attempt to hold the instrument down.

At approximately the same period in England, Daniel Dunglas Home was gaining a reputation as a psychic medium. He gave demonstrations at the Royal Courts of Napoleon III and Tsar Alexander II. His most celebrated feat took place on December 13, 1868, when, according to reliable witnesses, he was said to have levitated himself from a standing position, floated out of the room through a window and returned through another window in the house. Home was fully accepted by such thinkers as Sir Arthur Conan Doyle and William Crookes.

Physical mediumship is gaining ground today and many are starting to take it more seriously, but there is nothing new about it. A hundred years ago, Eusapia Palladino, a medium from Southern Italy, was performing demonstrations which convinced the most sceptical of thinkers. Dr Julien Ochoro-wicz, Director of the Institut General Psychologique in Paris, studied Palladino for several months in the early 1890s, and found that she could summon up a type of psychic twin. What-ever the theory, the facts remained clear—mind can be used to manipulate matter.

Another more notorious demonstrator of mind power was Rasputin who wielded great influence over the last Tsar and Tsarina and their family. Whether you regard him as a sinister and malevolent influence on the last members of the Romanoff dynasty or a much maligned, simple peasant with great powers, accounts abound of his powers of healing and indeed self-preservation. Reputedly he was very difficult to kill, and when a small group of self-appointed patriots decided to dis-pose of him, they were shocked, according to some accounts, to discover that it took several bullet shots to kill him, even though they were accurate. So remarkable, say these accounts, were his powers of mind, that he continued, for some time, to walk and talk when he should have been dead, causing fear and consternation among his assassins.

One could go on and on citing examples of mind over matter through history. The seeker after truth approaches any line of enquiry with a completely open mind. It is not a question of what should happen or what would make us comfortable if it happened; it is a question of what does happen. There is no doubt at all that exceptional occurrences are taking place, and have done throughout history, which reveal a power con-tained in mind which cannot be satisfactorily explained with-out looking beyond purely physical theories. You may not want to perform great demonstrations of mind over matter, but you probably do want to start to tap into higher mind to improve and enhance your life. To do this you need to tune into the mind vibrations which are all around us, and use them to help yourself.

8
Using Mind Vibrations

*

All life exists in different states of vibration. The difference between one person and another is their frequency of vibration—not just of the brain, but of the whole person. As science advances it moves increasingly towards the concept of frequency as an essential basis for explaining physical properties. It is also an essential concept in explaining the function of mind.

THE FIVE SENSES

Mind expresses itself through the five senses or qualities of life. Hindu philosophy tells us that these qualities, or *tattvas*, pervade all life and are used by the creative principle to bring differentiation. Plato said that when meditating it is necessary to extract the properties from objects and meditate on those properties rather than on the objects themselves. These properties are expressed through the qualities of life.

That is why it is so important how we use our senses. The whole function of our mind and its expression will be deeply affected by sense experience. Sight, sound, touch, taste and smell all play their part in expressing mind energy in a multitude of ways.

Psychics are people who have developed one or more of these five senses to the point where they can tune in and detect the higher vibrations associated with them. For example, clairvoyance is the ability of psychic vision. A clairvoyant can see the aura or energy which surrounds the physical body of a person and, by tuning into it, can learn about the person's physical and mental well-being. What she is really doing is translating the higher mind vibrations emitted by the person into a visual form. It is not physically visible because it is vibrating at a higher rate of frequency than physical matter.

The same is true of clairaudience (psychic hearing). Instead of using the visual sense, the psychic is using his sense of hearing to translate the higher mind vibrations into sound at a higher frequency than physical sound. Psychic touch can also be developed—for example, through the practice of healing—as well as psychic smell and even taste. The manifestation of different psychic senses will depend very much upon the individual and his or her feeling for different aspects. After all, it is all a question of attunement which comes from the feelings.

CHANGING VIBRATIONS

It is not necessary to be psychic, however, to become aware of and use mind vibrations—far from it. We all do this all the time. For example, moods are a result of mind vibrations of one kind or another. It may be a particular incident or thought which triggers off a mood, but this leads to a thought form or vibration which then surrounds you. On the other hand, you may develop a mood of one kind or another for no apparent reason. In reality you have, without realising it, tuned into a particular mind emanation which has affected you, either from a place or from people with whom you are associating.

The more you consider the concept of mind vibrations the

more you expand your consciousness about all things. Death no longer takes on the air of finality it once had for you. Okay, so the physical body dies—but what about the mind vibrations associated with the person? These are not physically tangible, they are beyond the physical organ of the brain, but they definitely exist. You have experienced them—and personal experience is the final test, not the objective findings of physical scientists, valuable though those can be.

This becomes a liberating philosophy: you can look anew at concepts such as the soul and strip away the superstitious myths surrounding them, analysing them as aspects of mind vibrations existing at a higher frequency than the physical body. More importantly, it is a philosophy you can use in practical ways. Mind vibrations not only exist, they can be changed for the good. Here are two exercises you can use to do this.

EXERCISE TEN: Changing Your Mood

Sit in a comfortable position, but for this exercise do not do any preparatory practices such as harmonious breathing. Instead, analyse what sort of mood you are in. You might be upset about something, generally fed up, bored or troubled in one way or another. That is the best time to do this exercise—when you want to change your mood into something better.

Remain sitting for a few minutes and observe your thoughts and emotions without making any attempt to change them. Then decide what sort of mood you want to be in. This may sound far-fetched, because we are led to believe that we are prisoners of our moods and emotions. A lot of psychological theories compound this limiting idea: we are told it all has to do with childhood traumas, suppressions and so on, which will never leave us. Rubbish! Everyone can change and by doing this exercise correctly you can prove it.

I should warn you that it can be very difficult to do and will require an effort of will, but it is well worth it. You may be feeling out of sorts when you do the exercise, or at best indifferent, and that is hardly the time when you feel like exerting yourself in a positive way, but it is certainly the most potent time to do it, exactly then: by the very act of doing it you are demonstrating the power of your mind over changing moods, and each time you do it, it will become easier. Gradually you will be able to change your moods and emotional reactions more easily in life in general, and this is a most valuable attribute, as well as being very good for your health and general well-being. Relatives, friends and associates will notice the change and will draw strength from you.

Do this exercise from time to time when your mood calls for it, but if you start you must finish. If you give up in the middle you will only undermine your willpower, which is the exact opposite of the result you want.

When you have analysed your mind, focus your concentration upon an image which symbolises for you joy, beauty, harmony, everything pleasant. It may be a place such as a beach, it may be a person you admire, it may be an event from the past which greatly uplifted you, such as a concert, play or outstanding demonstration of sporting skill. Whatever it is, it should be as uncomplicated as possible—just a simple image which has joyful connotations for you. This image should include several of the senses—for example, beautiful sounds or smells may mean more to you than visual images.

Having visualised this in your senses, start to allow the mood associated with the image to come to you. Try to feel it entering you—not the actual image but the association it has for you. Sometimes when you do this you can tangibly feel the emotions associated with the event. Be receptive, breathe rhythmically with your eyes closed and your hands palms downwards on the knees, and allow the vibrations to fill you. Then, focus again on your present life. This is most important because you do not want to live in the past, you just want the mind vibrations associated with the image. Retain those feelings you have invoked but return the focus of your concentration to present-day events. This brings a certain control to the exercise. Incidentally, do not use the same image too frequently but vary it. The idea is not to build up a fantasy about a particular image or event, but purely to use it and the associations it has for you to change your mood, and you will find if you make sufficient effort that it really does work.

EXERCISE ELEVEN:
Changing an Atmosphere

This is a similar exercise to the previous one, except that you are changing the atmosphere of a place rather than your own mood. Everywhere is imbued with mind vibrations of one kind or another. The psychometrist who uses psychic touch to analyse the mind vibrations in an object proves this beyond any doubt. Expert psychometrists have been able to identify precise details about objects which they did not know consciously, purely from tuning in to the vibrations contained in and around them. Antique dealers have been known to develop strange powers after years of examining ancient objects and discover details about antique pieces which they did not learn from study and experience. They attribute this to a mystical force of divination and call such a person a 'divvy'. In fact they are learning to tune in to the vibrations of objects and use their innate power to interpret them. In this exercise you are doing just that.

You have to be in a place where you want the atmosphere to change for the better. You may know a place where a pall hangs over it of unhappiness or general negativity. If you can, go there alone, sit down and perform harmonious breathing for a few moments. Then visualise an image of a place you love—this part of the exercise is very similar to the previous one. But this time, instead of allowing the mind vibrations to be drawn to you, draw them to the whole place you are trying to change. Visualise the place being filled with the vibrations you associate with the place you love. If your image is a classical concert, fill the place you are in with the sounds of this concert, in your mind's ear as it were. If there are smells of sea salt from your favourite ocean, fill this place with these smells.

You will be amazed what the power of creative visualisation can do in changing the vibrations of a place and altering the atmosphere to one of joy and hope. Do not tell others you have done this and see if they notice the change you have brought. They may not be sensitive to atmospheres but they may just say they feel better or happier than before.

This is not an easy exercise to do and you would be wise to perfect the previous exercise before embarking on this one, but with practice it really can work. As with the previous exercise, detach from the image you have visualised at the end of the exercise and focus on the place you are in instead, but now with a changed, far more positive atmosphere in it. You will find that by doing this, you become a person whom people want to have around because you will start naturally to be an uplifting presence wherever you go. We all know how marvellous nurses can be. They walk into a depressed, gloomy hospital ward full of sick people and change the atmosphere into a much lighter, more carefree and optimistic one. They are trained, of course, but they also learn to do this instinctively. They do not accept the negative atmosphere they find, but are determined to change it by radiating a different type of vibration. It really does work.

By doing this exercise you will start to become far more attuned to mind vibrations than ever before and be able to change them through your own positive thinking and creative visualisation.

THOUGHT FORMS

Really, mind vibrations are the result of thought patterns— they are in effect thought forms. In the book *Thought Forms* by Annie Besant and C. W. Leadbeater, a comparison is made of the music of Mendelssohn, Gounod and Wagner and the thought forms they emit. These thought forms are then illustrated in colour drawings to show the different effects they have. Besant and Leadbeater were both great mystics and used their clairvoyant powers to assess the mind emanations of these great classical composers, but the point they made is a very good one: sounds do more than entertain or uplift us. They are capable of creating real thought forms which will have their effect upon the atmosphere, even for those who do not hear the music itself.

Far-fetched as this may sound, the writings of certain theosophists in the early twentieth century developed this concept extensively: the idea that thought forms have an existence of their own and that, through colour or sound, mind energy can travel and affect thousands or even millions of people, most of whom are not consciously aware of the colour or sound impulses. In other words, the mind energy of the senses goes beyond their purely physical existence.

Cyril Scott, in his brilliant work *The Secret Influence of Music*, develops this theme further. He states that many of the great composers of the last three hundred years or more worked under the influence of a great Master in the Great White Brotherhood, an Order of Ascended Masters who it is claimed can live for hundreds or even thousands of years in the same body. They have been seen on various occasions throughout history, but they mainly work in seclusion in retreat, silently helping mankind without openly interfering with his culture. Their help is subtle and done through influence. One of these influences, says Cyril Scott, is the use of music, and the great composers were impressed by a particular Master in this secret spiritual order to bring about specific changes to the culture of the world. For example, Beethoven came to introduce a humanitarian consciousness, Chopin a certain refinement and Wagner a high expression of true love. All these composers, says Scott, used music as a form of energy, but their real intent was to produce an influence on the thought pattern of the world and hence bring about change for the good, even for those who never heard the music.

Musical experiments have been done with plants, in which various kinds of music were played to them. It was found that certain types of music enhance the growth of plants and other kinds stunt their growth. For example, heavy rock music is not good for plants, whereas Baroque music and certain forms of New Age music are good for them. These experiments have had staggeringly consistent results and some experimenters have even been able to identify particular composers who are beneficial to plants. Nobody is suggesting that the plants enjoy a particular tune, but the energy experienced by them when exposed to certain types of music has a definite effect. Those readers who have pets know how much they too can be affected by different kinds of music and sound.

A smell can change an atmosphere completely, for better or for worse. It is not just the power of the aroma, wonderful though this may be, it is the energies which are brought into the mind when the aroma pervades an atmosphere. People eat foods not just for sensory enjoyment or dietary reasons. Certain types of food have mental associations for them. Although it is not highly developed at this time and is often associated with self-indulgence, taste too can be developed to enhance our mental awareness and appreciation of all life.

Many books have been written about touch and the effect that it has on our mind, particularly in the areas of healing and health. Physical contact can also be extremely important for people in counselling and bereavement. Of course, many theories exist about the benefits or otherwise of sexual encounters, and there is no question that this has a profound effect upon the mind as well as the body. The sense of touch can be used to enhance and heal or it can be overindulged and lead to dissipation and the reduction of your mental powers.

COLOUR

Of all the senses, the one you can use the most easily if you are fortunate to have your sight is the sense of colour. Those who are blind often learn to develop some of the other senses, particularly sound, above the norm and thereby compensate to some degree for the loss of the sense of sight. From the point of view of mind development, the sense of sight is the most readily usable because so many creative visualisations have been devised using it. The power of imagination through visualising colour is one of the most potent weapons in the armoury of mental development, and for this reason I shall discuss it in some detail. We should remember, however, that it would be theoretically possible to use any of the other senses, and indeed in the future there will undoubtedly be more work done on sound, smell, taste and touch visualisation exercises.

Colour affects all our lives, both physically and metaphysically. A colourless or excessively introverted person can use colour to project her personality; a dull and tedious job can be enhanced by a colourfully decorated office; even a meal can be greatly enhanced by the use of different-coloured ingredients. This is particularly advantageous if you are on a rather severe diet which is bland and boring: colour can be used to help to bring it to life. Mystics say that all our thoughts are expressed in colour. They say that around us is a force field known as the aura, composed of psychic or etheric matter which can be seen by a clairvoyant as manifesting in a multitude of different colours. Through clairvoyantly seeing these colours, the mind of a person can be known.

Some say that an appreciation of the importance of colour goes back at least as far as ancient Egypt, where the influence of colour could be seen in the great temples and wisdom schools such as those at Karnak and Thebes. Reputedly, certain parts of their buildings were set aside as colour halls, so that the effects of different colour vibrations could be studied and applied.

Manuscripts left by ancient Egyptian priests are said to show a system of colour science which had much in common with mystical teachings from the east and western occult philosophy. A correspondence was seen between the sevenfold nature of man, the seven planes of existence and the sevenfold division of the light spectrum. The seven major colours or rays are red, orange, yellow, green, blue, indigo and violet. Each one represented certain powerful attributes for the student to aspire to. Some mystical schools concentrated specifically on the three primary colours of red, yellow and blue, taking them to represent the body, mind and spirit respectively.

Of course, these colours are only the visible part of the light spectrum, and if we were able to know the entire spectrum we would then have some idea of the totality of creation which in its purest form is just light. As the Master Aetherius, a Spiritual Being who communicates telepathically through Dr

George King, pointed out, all matter in the solar system is really just solidified sunlight. We owe our complete experience cycle on all levels to the sun, which is why many so-called primitive civilisations have worshipped this ever-shining, all-powerful orb. Were they really so primitive to regard this as a Holy Being? In my view, not at all.

Colours can be used in many ways to enhance your life. Clothing, lighting, the decoration of your home or office, even the colour of your car, will affect your mood and general feeling. Colours are frequently used in everyday language to denote different moods. 'Singing the blues' or 'feeling blue' are phrases taken to denote sadness. Actually blue is not a colour of sadness, but of coolness, calmness, passivity which in a negative phase could be interpreted in that way.

'He saw red' denotes anger, and red is a colour of stimulation, vibrancy, which can include anger among its emotions.

'He is in a brown study' is used to denote a mood of abstract indifference, when a person is lost in his thoughts. Brown is not a positive, dynamic colour, but rather a distant one, and the colour is used to describe this distant mood.

Of course, not all the phrases which are used with colours describe the true mental energies which come from the colour. For example, 'green with envy' is not representative of the colour green which is a vibration of balance, harmony and healing. To describe somebody as 'yellow', meaning cowardly, is again not particularly appropriate for this colour. Yellow is actually the colour of mental ability and should not necessarily imply cowardice. Some others, though, are very interesting. For example, the phrase 'purple prose' to describe literature which is rich in descriptive terminology and high emotion does have something in common with the colour purple which is associated with spirituality and advancement in all forms. Indeed, the colour purple is understood both in royal and ecclesiastical circles to denote something very special, with mystical or divine attributes.

In healing, where a colour lamp or slide projector is used to apply different colours to people's anatomy, the effects can be measured sometimes with startling results. There are cases, for example, of people with inflammation or swelling who have witnessed their affliction physically diminish beneath the effects of a blue light. Blue, after all, is the cooling colour and the exact opposite of red which is associated with inflammation.

Studies have been done into the psychology of colour and it has been found that people of a certain type of character tend to use one colour more than another. This is not necessarily a good thing. Just because you like a colour, it doesn't always mean that this is the colour you need. For example, if you are a hypertense and anxious person, you might need the cooling vibrations of a blue piece of clothing or decoration in your home, although you may in fact be attracted to the bright colours which correspond to your mood. If you are a lethargic, melancholy type, you may well wish to put on red or orange clothing to brighten up your day. There are colour co-ordinators who give detailed advice on helping people find clothing and decor to suit their moods and needs as well as just their taste.

Although it can be extremely smart, black is not a colour which contains any of the positive attributes of mind emanations from the colour rays. It is a deadener from a mental point of view and has no therapeutic qualities. Understandably, it is associated with death and may help some people to identify with their bereavement, but it will definitely not help them to change their mood and get over the grief they are suffering. The colour grey very accurately describes moods and people. A grey person is someone who is dull, uninteresting and lacking in the vitality which colour brings. It is not a deadener in the same way as black, but more a boring, tedious vibration. It symbolises indifference and mediocrity. If a politician is called grey, it means that he is too ordinary to qualify for a top job. Again, grey can be a smart colour to wear, but not a radiant colour with beneficial mind emanations.

White is taken to symbolise purity, a spiritual vocation and heavenliness. White, of course, contains all the colours of the spectrum and it is correct to say that there is a certain completeness and perfection about it. It does not, however, specifically promote any particular kind of mental energy.

As well as using colours in physical life, you can also use them in your mental life. One of the simplest ways to do this is through a simple colour breathing exercise using visualisation. The following is a safe, simple but effective one to use:

EXERCISE TWELVE:
Colour Breathing Exercise

Sit comfortably in a chair and for a few minutes make sure that you are completely relaxed with the spine erect but without any tension in the shoulders. Relax your mind and start to observe thoughts as they come and go into the brain in a rhythm or wave motion. As you do so, start to breathe deeply, gradually lengthening the breath but making it as rhythmic as you possibly can. Then start to visualise a beautiful, gentle, mid-spectrum green light surrounding you completely. Do not visualise this entering you through the nostrils on your breath, but rather in a more indirect way as if the process of breathing is drawing this green light to you. Do not use any colour other than green because you want to be absolutely sure that you are harmonising yourself and certain colours are not conducive to this exercise.

Providing that you always stay with the simple green light surrounding you and permeating you gently for a few minutes, this exercise should restore some balance and harmony to your being. It can be done after some practice wherever you are, but you must be sure always to stay with the same colour of mid-spectrum green. This will only be effective if you are able to visualise the colour correctly. Not all people are as good as others at visualising colours, and it may be necessary for you to have a piece of paper or some other object which has this colour on it, so that you can observe this for some time and get used to the colour in your mind until you are able to visualise it at will. This is a harmonising, relaxing practice, which should only be done for a few minutes at a time. It will bring greater peace, balance and good health to you. It does not need to be practised too often—once or twice a week would be quite sufficient, or whenever you feel the need.

9

Awaken Your Higher Mind

*

Very little has been written about the most elevated aspect of mind: the superconscious. Perhaps it is because those who have really discovered this wonderful part of our inner self have usually held their own counsel about it, apart from confiding in a few chosen students. The superconscious mind is that part of the mind which is literally above the normal conscious state and which produces higher states of consciousness, deep intuition and psychic awareness.

EXAMPLES OF HIGHER CONSCIOUSNESS

Of the many reported examples in history of those who entered deeper states of consciousness, here are some of the most exceptional. Blaise Pascal, who lived in seventeenth-century France, is best known for his outstanding contribution to geometry, science, mathematical formulae and theology. He was and still is regarded as one of the greatest minds of that century. Towards the end of his life he abandoned the world and devoted himself to religious and charitable concerns. He lived almost as a recluse, and it was only after his death that one of his writings was found by his servant on a folded parchment. It became known as *Pascal's Mystic Amulette* and the following are extracts from it:

> From about half-past ten in the evening until about half-past twelve, midnight, FIRE. God of Abraham, God of Isaac, God of Jacob, not of the philosophers nor of the Wise. Assurance, joy, assurance, feeling, joy, peace, God of Jesus Christ, my God and thy God. Thy God shall be my God. Forgotten of the world and of all except God . . . Just Father, the world has not known thee but I have known thee. Joy, joy, joy, tears of joy. I do not separate myself from thee . . . Continual joy for the days of my life on earth. I shall not forget what you have taught me. Amen.

Of course this experience is couched in theological terminology familiar to Pascal and his contemporaries, but it resembles closely similar mystic experiences enjoyed in the East: a discovery of oneness with the divine bringing bounteous joy.

William Wordsworth had a very different concept of divinity, one which drew him considerable orthodox disapproval, even in later years, from his old friend, Samuel Taylor Coleridge. Wordsworth saw a divinity and oneness in all things, especially nature, and expressed this in his poetry. He also expressed the illumination he had obviously experienced in higher states of consciousness. In his lines written at Tintern Abbey at the end of the eighteenth century he wrote:

> . . . that serene and blessed mood,
> In which the affections gently lead us on,
> Until, the breath of this corporeal frame
> And even the motion of our human blood
> Almost suspended, we are laid asleep
> In body, and become a living soul:
> While with an eye made quiet by the power

Of harmony, and the deep power of joy,
We see into the life of things.

Wordsworth had obviously experienced what is described in mystical circles as the opening of the third eye to be able to detail this mood or state of consciousness so accurately.

More recently the nineteenth-century American poet Walt Whitman described ecstatic states of mental power and inspiration. He wrote the following in an edition of the *Leaves* in 1855:

> Swiftly arose and spread around me the peace and joy
>   and knowledge that pass all the art and argument of
>   the earth;
> And I knew that the hand of God is the elder hand of
>   my own,
> And I know that the spirit of God is the eldest brother
>   of my own,
> And that all the men ever born are also my brothers,
> . . . and the women my sisters and lovers,
> And that a kelson of creation is love.

Some who have experienced the highest states of consciousness say that they are beyond verbal description. The great sage Shri Ramakrishna, who lived in India at the end of the nineteenth century, talked of the attainment of the highest states of superconscious awareness in this way. He said that it could be compared to a person who had managed to climb a wall and see over the other side. Another person standing behind him could see only his expression of sheer delight as he witnessed the scene over the wall and hear his gasp of joy before he jumped over. This look of sheer delight and the gasp of joy were enough to convince the watcher that he too should climb the self-same wall.

INTUITION

The subject of the innate psychic powers we can all tap if we choose to do so is a vast one which I have covered in my book *Unlock Your Psychic Powers*. But of all the faculties of ESP that can be attained and demonstrated, there is no doubt in my mind that the most valuable is the faculty of intuition.

We often use intuition, whether we realise it or not. The hunch, or the impression about someone or something which causes us to act in a certain way, is a typical example. Sometimes you might scarcely realise you are getting an intuitive impulse, but will just act almost on instinct, as it were. If you were to analyse more carefully you would find that very often you have been led by this intuitive part of your inner self which is starting to open the door to higher mind.

While the subconscious is a functional part of our mind, the superconscious is that part which leads us to the most elevated, inspirational realisations. Some people refer to the superconscious part of our being as our soul. When you have an experience which you feel comes from your very soul, this can be the prompting of your superconscious mind.

All too often people ignore this higher part of their mind, not out of any sense of wickedness, as some orthodox religions might suggest, but because they are too preoccupied with mundane and materialistic matters. We use our conscious mind to govern our lives to the point where we are almost dictated to by it. To some extent, we can learn to tap into the subconscious mind and bring forward the rich storehouse of information that lies there. But the superconscious mind seems to be treated as the last option, the one we use if we have time to spare. This is a big mistake because we can rob ourselves of the use of our most precious innate mental faculty of all.

Higher mind is that faculty within us which prompts us to achieve important things for others as well as ourselves. It is that part of our mind that wants to help, love and care for others. It wants to be truthful and wants to reveal the real answers to life's purpose. We can penetrate the deepest mysteries through the superconscious until knowledge within us is recognised at a conscious level. The whole transition into enlightenment is a transition from consciousness to superconsciousness.

The ability to move from the beta brain wave state into the alpha brain wave state is an essential preparation for higher consciousness, but it is not the whole story. It gives you the opportunity to observe yourself because in the alpha state of consciousness it is far easier to come to terms with your real self, who you are, what you feel, and to get a balanced perspective on life. The beta state is activity, pressure, drive, with a multitude of different thoughts, tending to stimulate you to further and further activity. Slowing down this brain wave motion, and slowing down with it the flow of adrenalin through the physiological system, brings as its reward a certain tranquillity and calmness which allows you to focus on exactly where you are at, not only intellectually but on a deeper emotional level. To journey into a higher mind, though, you need to do more than this. Some books on meditation make the mistake of seeing the tranquil state produced by alpha wave motion as the final goal in itself. Certainly it will enable you to improve your health and gain more inner control over your materialistic life, but if you wish to go farther and make the journey into deeper realisation, you will have to perform exercises in mind development to pluck the fruits of your higher self.

What you are really doing when you make this journey into supermind is not so much changing your thought patterns as changing your level of being. It is all about being, rather than just thinking or doing. When you go into a discotheque with flashing lights, where people are inebriated and dancing in a carefree, highly excited manner, you can immediately feel the powerful energies that exist there. Because people are letting their hair down and are generally in a relaxed state, the energies within them can flow freely outwards. This does not mean that they are going to attain a high level of consciousness—in fact, that is probably the exact opposite of what most of them wish to do. They want to have fun, relax, unwind and maybe find a sexual partner. These energies can be experienced quite easily by anyone who walks in; you feel them tangibly, and if you are in that kind of mood, you will like them. It is not just the music or the visual effect of the lighting and the dancing, it is the vibration of the place, as I described in the previous chapter.

If, on the other hand, you walk into a Buddhist temple where monks are in the process of practising ancient Sanskrit mantra—which they have performed for many years and have attained a high level of spirituality through doing so—you will feel entirely different energies. Again, there is a lot of magnetism present, but this time it is directed towards an entirely different goal. Here also a certain relaxation has taken place because the monks will have learnt meditative techniques which enable them to find peace; but their focus, instead of being on excitement, sexuality, pleasure and emotional release is on spiritualisation, oneness, harmony and love. The two could not be more different.

The purpose of making this comparison is not to be judgemental in any way, but to illustrate the tangible difference in the energies which are emitted. That really is what the journey into higher mind is all about. It is a journey of changing your energy flow.

INSPIRATION

Inspiration is the highest expression of mind. It is something which can appear to come haphazardly, initially as a feeling more than a thought, although the seed of that feeling is generally translated into some form of thought expression. Beet-

hoven's great frustration was not so much becoming inspired
and hearing in his mind's ear, as it were, the sounds he wished
to convey to the world, but translating these sounds into per-
formable music. This was, of course, compounded by his deaf-
ness. He had to put on paper and translate, with known
musical instruments, the ethereal sounds he had experienced.
For the inspirational process to be complete, it must be made
manifest.

It seems obvious that when you are in an inspired mood
you are far more capable of writing, painting, inventing or
whatever other focus you have for your inspiration. But have
you ever considered that this inspired mood is not a haphazard
thing? It is a state of being which reflects your vibrations at
that time. It may have been caused by any number of things.
Some people are inspired by incense, some people by music,
some people by the countryside and others by the sea. You
have to discover what inspires you. It may be the sun, the
stars, the cosmos itself. The sight of a great waterfall, a mountain peak, the fresh air that you breathe in certain country
districts, the sound of a nightingale—all of these things have
inspired people.

If you wish to enter higher mind, you will have to develop
your faculty of inspiration and there are many ways to do
that. If you have in your life a combination of peace and
inspiration, the two great forces which seem diametrically
opposed and yet are perfectly balanced, then you will be able
to unravel the mysteries of your higher consciousness. These
two forces of inner peace and higher inspiration are very well
illustrated by the difference between East and West. In the
past the East has been associated with a reflective, contemplative life for those who wish to turn to the mystical or religious
path. In the West, on the other hand, the poets, artists and
scientists have used their inspiration to express sublime feelings and thoughts. More and more nowadays, a merging is
taking place of Eastern and Western concepts. That is one of

the hallmarks of the real New Age movement, which draws upon ancient Eastern practices as freely as it promotes humanitarian actions. You need a detachment from everyday materialistic concerns in order to switch your focus into higher mind.

SELF-IMPROVEMENT

We all fall into the trap of thinking that we are far too busy to spend time on ourselves. This can appear to be a very unselfish attitude, but is it really? We become so tensed up and obsessed with the minor details of everyday living that we are dull company, with grey, uninteresting personalities—in short, uninspired. Have we really been unselfish?

The quest for higher mind demands that we spend some time on self-improvement. Some will turn to one or more of the systems of yoga to do this. I personally have practised various forms of yoga for many years and thoroughly recommend them. In particular, Mantra Yoga will definitely heighten your vibrations if you practise it regularly and with love in your heart. The giving of spiritual healing will also heighten your vibrations as will the practice of prayer for the world as a whole. Pranayama (breathing exercises) is also an extremely helpful way of developing higher consciousness because you are drawing into yourself a stream of living energies which will cause the vibration of your body and aura to be changed for the good.

The company you mix with will definitely affect your state of vibration. If you wish to attain higher mind you should associate with others who are also interested in such things, so that the vibrations will rub off on each other. Those who are actively opposed to all things mystical and metaphysical will detune you if you spend too much time in their company. Of course, it can be unavoidable at times to do so; it may be a necessary part of your work. But associating with those who are at least sympathetic to your desire for higher consciousness will help your quest.

The places you visit are also very important. If you walk into some buildings which have been used for religious or mystical purposes you can feel the atmosphere immediately. It will change you. And if you visit a 'dive' inhabited by drug addicts, criminals and the like, you will sense a very different atmosphere and will be changed by that, too. It is a very good test to walk into a building and try to tune in to the atmosphere there and see what you feel. The pursuit of higher mind is to seek out, wherever possible, higher vibrations so that you can raise your own energy level.

Your visual and reading matter will have a great effect on your level of consciousness, far more than just for the day you see or read it. It will stay with you for some time afterwards. Incidents are recorded in which certain types of extremely aggressive and negative rock music have caused people to behave in bizarre and sometimes dangerous ways. This is due not just to the lyrics of the songs but to the vibrations they create. On the other hand, there are those who have been so elevated by certain pieces of music that they have been inspired to change their lives for the better. You should never underestimate the influence of the mind belt around you. If you wish to seek out higher mind, you must expose yourself as often as possible to the influence that will lead you there.

We cannot avoid the whole issue of religion when talking about higher mind. This is obviously a very personal thing and one which evokes a mixed bag of emotions. Nevertheless, it would be broadly true to say that most people of a strong religious faith will say that they have been helped greatly by their religion, that they have been given strength from it to enable them to get through the difficult times in their lives. What this religion has done through their faith, conviction, belief or inner realisation has been to enable them to draw on some part of their own higher mind. It is not, after all, enough just to read the Ten Commandments, or lines from the Dham-mapada, the Hindu Scripts or the Koran. You have to have a belief in it and the strength to carry it out. We all know that certain orthodox religions have misled people by encouraging them to take up arms and fight, but that is not the point I am making here. Generally speaking, the exposure to the vibrations of a religious path will help to strengthen people, even if only to a very small degree. I do not include in this those people who follow religious paths purely out of fear or guilt, but those who have a sincere and deeply held religious conviction. Some humanitarians who believe in the value of life itself, the beauty of the universe and creation could also be said to be religious, although they might not regard them-selves as such.

Above all, higher mind is compassion for others. Have you ever noticed that when you do something to help another, for no personal reward, you feel good? This feeling is an inner impulse being satisfied. Indeed, happiness is really a satisfied conscience. No matter how wealthy or powerful you might be, if your conscience is not satisfied, you cannot really be happy. The mirage of materialism suggests that pleasure can be measured in terms of material acquisition. In that case pleasure is something far removed from joy. There are many examples of wise but not wealthy people who have discovered far more joy in their lives than those who have it all materially but do not feel good inside. This good feeling, which comes from the release of human compassion, is the hallmark of higher mind.

Those people who have expressed fantastic capabilities of inspirational mind power earn the description of 'genius'. And yet so often the geniuses of history have displayed overt weak-nesses in their private lives, and they include many great composers, artists, writers, scientists, politicians and others who have had a decisive impact on the direction of cultures. Why is this? One reason is that the same force which enhances the inspirational faculty in a person enhances all his other faculties as well. Unless he has displayed the type of balanced control described in Part One of this book, he would be more prone than normal to the desires and passions which can take on an exaggerated or distorted expression. The old adage 'all power corrupts' should really be altered to 'all power corrupts unless you do something about it'. If you have mind control, it will not corrupt, it will only enhance. But if you do nothing to control the increased mental powers you are gaining, then they will tend to magnify everything within you, whether it be good, bad or indifferent. Here I must stress the importance of mastering the techniques of mind control described in Part One of this book before you move on to develop the higher mind.

CONTEMPLATION

Higher mind is all about feeling. When you go beyond the stage of pure concentration and start to introduce feeling and respond to what you are concentrating on internally, then you are entering a contemplative state. It is then that you realise from personal experience that the consciousness of man is more than the molecular structure in his head. It involves his whole being. When you take the step beyond concentration into contemplation, you not only focus your mind on an object but you also respond to the feelings and emotions which virtually come from the object of your contemplation. This is the step into higher mind which can lead you into areas of deep intuitive awareness.

In his audio cassette lecture, 'Concentration, Contemplation, Meditation', Dr King describes brilliantly the difference between these three state of consciousness. He explains that concentration taken to its zenith will enable you to know all there is to know about a particular subject. Through the application of single-minded concentration you will be able to deduce all the details appertaining to a particular subject and work out how they all fit in.

Contemplation will take you on to the next stage. Through deep contemplation you can learn things about a subject which are not accessible to the conscious mind. This is where your intuition starts to develop and, like anything else, the more you exercise it the better it will work for you. You will never develop a sound intuition unless you start to use it regularly. Through contemplation, says Dr King, you can know not only the facts but the mind vibrations behind those facts. You can start to understand the motivations of any people concerned, some of the background to events which have not been fully revealed, and so on. An intuitive look at history, for example, can provide you with a very different picture than the facts available in textbooks. In fact a good historian does develop her intuition, whether she realises it or not. She may put it down to knowledge and deduction, but very often she is contemplating past events and gleaning information at an intuitive level which throws completely new light on the subject. So often, all we know about history is the equivalent of official releases at the time or gossip and rumour, no more reliable than some popular press reports are today. A developed intuition through the practice of contemplation, which is a very different thing from guesswork, will enable you to read accurately between the lines and draw out much more information than was accessible through concentration alone.

On the topic of meditation Dr King is unequivocal. His idea of this sublime state is far removed from some of the meditation practices which are taught so freely nowadays. This is the state where your mind is bathed in the light of superconsciousness, says Dr King, and at its deepest level you can know all that there is to know about whatever you meditate upon. This meditative knowledge goes beyond the subject virtually to an abstract level and tells you why as well as how this subject came into being in its present form. This is the deepest aspect of supermind and one I shall refer to again in the last chapter. I must also state clearly that I myself have not entered the deepest states of meditation, so I can only pass on what those few Masters who have done so have shared with us.

But first things first. You will never enter true meditative states until you have first learnt to contemplate with a high degree of success. The following is an exercise which will help you to learn contemplation.

EXERCISE THIRTEEN:
Contemplating an Object

For the purposes of this exercise select an object of beauty or significance. A religious artefact or a work of art would be ideal. Alternatively, it could be an antique item which you treasure, a photograph of an impressive building or some other object of admiration, which is nevertheless impersonal. It should not have nostalgic or sentimental attachments for you, because these will interfere with the exercise.

Start by harmonising your breathing, as in Exercise Two (p. 39), for this is an excellent preparation for all metaphysical practices. Place the object in front of you, at eye level if possible. Having breathed rhythmically and deeply for a few minutes, focus your concentration on the selected object. Note its features from a technical as well as an aesthetic point of view. Having done this for a while, start to relax your mind and instead of concentrating on the features of the object, observe your own thought processes. By concentrating on the object, you have established it as a focus for your mind. Now start to observe your thought processes at work—that is, your own thoughts about the object. This is not always easy to do, but with practice you will master it. The trick is to maintain your mental focus upon the object but observe your own reactions at the same time. In a way you move from an active into a more receptive state.

If you continue this you will start to receive not only thoughts but also feelings about the object, as though you are really getting to know it from the inside. You may even get psychic impressions about it. Taken far enough, you feel a certain oneness with the object and really gain a deep insight into it. This is very deep contemplation and can lead into higher states of consciousness. Do not allow your focus to drift away from the object at any stage, although you may be tempted to do so by any number of distractions. The initial concentration will be invaluable in this respect in establishing the focus, but you will have to maintain it throughout to get the best results from your contemplation.

You will find that regularly practising contemplation, every week if possible, will naturally develop your intuitive powers and you will gain a deeper insight into whatever you focus upon.

10

Magnetising Yourself With Natural Energies

*

Through practising contemplation and understanding higher mind you start to realise that all life is contained in a virtual sea of energy. As science delves into the minutiae of subatomic particles which constantly bombard each other in patterns and rhythms of frenzied activity, hence creating movement, manifestation and material existence, it raises more and more questions about what lies behind. What exactly is directing this?

POWERS OF ANIMALS

If you examine the animal kingdom, you cannot fail to be amazed by the ability for survival you see there. The instinct of self-preservation goes beyond chance. It is directed, it cannot be purely the result of some haphazard form of natural selection as proposed in the Darwinian concept of evolution. There is a mind controlling the creatures of this world. Is it an individual mind or is it a group consciousness or is it both? These are issues which throw light upon the energy that governs all life—an energy which is dictated by some form of mind.

Animals have been known to demonstrate extraordinary powers and numerous incidents are on record to illustrate this. One typical example happened to me as a young boy. We moved house from a village near Abingdon in Berkshire to Sevenoaks in Kent, more than 120 miles away, taking our family cat with us. Soon after we had settled in we went on holiday. The cat must have thought that we had returned to our former home and was seen in that Berkshire village again some weeks later. Even more amazing than that was the fact that, after our return from the holiday, the cat made its way back to Sevenoaks and found its new home again.

Animals have demonstrated remarkable abilities and one of these was Missie, the psychic dog of Denver, who became very famous in the 1970s. She was able to interpret numbers in front of many witnesses. She would be tested on the numbers of letters in a word and invariably gave the correct answer by barking the appropriate number of times. She was even reputed to make predictions accurately on election results and other matters through the number of her barks. According to one report, there was a doctor who was very sceptical of Missie's powers and not willing to be convinced. The dog's owner said, 'Well, doctor, there is one number that neither Missie nor I know and that is your private home number.' The doctor stated that he had never given this telephone number to anyone. When Missie barked out the doctor's private number he became a convinced believer.

There are many such stories of the psychic powers of animals. More valuable are the attempts by psychics to commune with animals and help them. One such animal psychic recounted how she had communicated with a racehorse which was not co-operating with its owner and was refusing to run in races. The psychic, who claimed to have a telepathic rapport with animals, communed with the horse and learned that it had not received its usual rest period when it was put out to a stable to rest. On questioning the owner of the horse about this, the owner said that it certainly had had a rest period, but the horse still informed the psychic mentally that it had not rested properly. The owner then contacted the stable concerned and found that they had been racing the horse there, which should not have been the case. The psychic was then able to communicate to the horse and promise it that if it did one more race for the owner it would have a proper rest period. The horse then co-operated, ran the race, and, sure enough, received a proper rest period.

Stories such as these abound. I am sure that many who are reading this and have pets to whom they are close will identify with this type of bond. I myself have found that talking gently to my own cat about what I am doing and explaining things which upset him, such as my professional requirement to travel away for periods of time, has brought a newfound understanding and peace of mind to the cat. Many people talk to their animals and believe that they do indeed get a response. I am not suggesting here that there is a language communication taking place but that something in the energy of one's communication is received by the animal and interpreted at that level.

PLANTS AND ENERGY

This ability to communicate also applies to the plant kingdom. Experiments have shown that if plants are blessed they prosper, if they are cursed they wither and die. Again, it is not that the plants are able to understand intellectually the difference between a blessing or a curse, it is the energy behind these thought forms which causes a reaction in the plants. There are people who, even today, attribute healing powers to trees. In small villages, including those in the Dutch province of Brabant, it is reportedly still possible to find a 'fever tree', an oak whose branches hang full of shreds of cloth which have been knotted there. They are pieces torn from the clothing or sheets of sick people. The healing strength of the tree is said to pass into the shreds and from there link up through the vibrations in the clothing or sheets with the sick people. It is a system of magic which is said to have definite results. If so, it is certainly evidence of the responsiveness of plant life to mind emanations.

ENVIRONMENT AND ENERGY

And of course, it is true of humans. We are very responsive to the mind emanations we receive in different environments. People who live under extremely aggressive conditions, even if the aggression is not being directed at them personally but is in the atmosphere, are more prone to physical ailments. Some will say this is a purely psychosomatic phenomenon, by which they mean that it is an intellectual reaction to what they are experiencing. But such a theory does not explain those people who experience the effects of natural energies when they are not consciously aware of the emanations they are receiving.

For example, a friend and I decided to take up the practice of yoga while we were at university. We rented an apartment together and every night performed certain yoga practices, including healing, mantra and other beneficial exercises. When we moved into this flat the owner was a rather morose, dejected individual. Gradually, over the months that we were performing our nightly practices of yoga and meditation exercises, the owner, who lived downstairs, started to change. Having been extremely lethargic, he suddenly became active. He decided to decorate the entire building and could even be heard singing as he went about his self-appointed work!

On the other hand there are those who have lived in depressing environments who have found themselves becoming depressed even though they have not been aware consciously that others in their environs were in a negative frame of mind. They were conditioning the natural energies with their negativity. There are ways of protecting yourself against this and the following exercise will help:

EXERCISE FOURTEEN:
Self-Protection Practice

If you are in the company of depressed or angry people, you can protect yourself from the energies they are emitting. First of all you have to decide whether you need to be there at all. In some cases it might be necessary—for example, you might be visiting somebody in hospital who needs your help. You do not, however, wish to receive the negative energies of ill health into your being because that way you will not be able to help the patient; you will instead come down to his or her level of unhappiness, depression or illness. In a case like this you can practise this exercise, which is very simple and yet very effective.

Take a few rhythmic deep breaths, and on the in-breath draw into yourself—not just through the nostrils, but through the whole of your body and mind, which is around the body—a white light. Visualise yourself being impregnated with this white light and virtually surrounded by it. This very simple exercise, if done on each occasion when you encounter negative vibrations, will bring a protection to you; it will lift you up mentally and spiritually and prevent these emanations from reaching you.

You can do this quickly; nobody in the room need even know that you are doing it. As a side effect, it can lead to others in the room receiving healing from you or from the energy that you have drawn to yourself. Be sure, though, at all times that this is a pure white energy and draw it into your virtually as you breathe in. As you breathe out, allow yourself to feel calm and cleansed, but on the in-breath draw this white light to you until it surrounds the whole of your body from top to bottom.

Even an inanimate object such as a piece of machinery responds to the feelings and energies which are transmitted to it. Some people talk to their car and swear blind that when the car has broken down, a few encouraging words make all the difference. Laugh as some people might, stories such as this occur too frequently to be ignored. Once again this proves that mind is not purely an intellectual process or even a subconscious process alone—it is an interaction of energy.

NATURAL ENERGIES

So what is this energy? Ancient Sanskrit writings, going back many thousands of years, describe the existence of a universal life force called *Prana*. They believed that the Creator brought into being this energy which in different modes of manifestation expressed itself in different ways. The power which governed this expression was the power of mind. Universal mind governed all life throughout creation and individuals were only virtual particles of mind manifesting in different ways. They believed in one great whole and that each cell in the body of that whole affects the whole to some degree.

In studying the mind, we can draw heavily on this idea of universal life force or energy which pervades all things and which is conditioned by mind. It has been known by many names, including *chi* as in the practice of T'ai Chi and *ki* as in Aikido. Of course, this concept in no way negates individual responsibility or identity, but it does show the immense potential of drawing upon that aspect or frequency of mind energy we require at any particular time. There is no shortage of energy, only our use of it may be lacking.

All this may sound rather abstract and irrelevant to everyday life unless you apply it to actual situations. When you listen to rock music, you are drawing to yourself a certain type of energy. You are starting to tune in to a frequency of thought which is manifested in the music. This brings that type of energy into your life and if you listen to rock music frequently enough, then the natural energies will be conditioned with that type of thought. They will start to pervade your life and you will become a rock thinker. You will behave in accordance with the ideas and the energies behind this music. Similarly, if you engross yourself in romantic literature, full of emotional interchanges between men and women with great emphasis laid upon the sentimentality of love-making, you will attract to yourself those kinds of energies. You will start to think in that way and this too will affect your behaviour. If you decide to expose yourself to patterns of thought which are positive, uplifting and enthusiastic, you will start to attract those energies into your life and even into your character.

It is very important, therefore, that we choose very carefully, as far as we can, what energies we wish to be exposed to. This does not mean becoming puritanical and running away from all negative influences, but it does mean gaining a control over the effect energy influences have upon you.

These natural energies are a pure living source of power which you can draw on freely and which does not diminish. On the contrary, the more you use it, the more it will naturally flow to you. The more you send out to others, the more you will get back. It is contained in the food you eat and the liquid you drink. One reason for having fresh, organic food and drink is because it will be far more charged with these natural energies than processed equivalents. This is not the only reason, but it is a very important one. If you drink water from a mountain brook, providing it is safe to do so, you will find that it is far more invigorating and energising than bottled water. This is caused by the energies contained in the natural environment of the moment and the friction between molecules as the waters flow freely down the mountainside.

YOGA BREATHING

The most immediate and accessible way to magnetise yourself with natural breathing is the practice of Pranayama or Yoga Breathing. Ancient Hindu writings venerated correct breathing as the most sacred and powerful practice anyone could perform. They believed that tremendous powers could be attained through performing specific breathing exercises at certain times. They stated that there are five major *pranas* and five minor *pranas*, or energies, emitted by the sun at certain times and that each of these have certain attributes. If you could discover when the type of energy you required was flowing, you could draw it to you on the breath that you breathed and this would enable you to attain your goals.

Of course the systems worked out by these yogis thousands of years ago were applicable to very different cultural conditions. The technological revolution and the stresses and strains that go with it have radically altered the type of practice which can safely and effectively be used today. It is wise when seeking out a system of pranayama to turn to a modern teacher who understands the requirements of living in today's world. I have used the system published by Dr King in his book *Contact Your Higher Self Through Yoga* and have found it to be indispensable.

When practising breathing exercises, you must always remember that it is not the oxygen you are seeking to draw to you, it is the natural energies carried on and through the oxygen. You can use creative visualisation greatly to potentise the energies you draw to yourself and thereby magnetise yourself. This, in turn, enables you to dispense those energies naturally to others, even though you may not be consciously aware that you are doing so. You automatically become a far more magnetic and dynamic person to be with.

It has been discovered that it is far more effective in terms of self-magnetisation to breathe through the nostrils separately than both together. When dealing with practices like this you learn to deal with actualities rather than theories. In this respect there are similarities with homoeopathy. Some medical practitioners dismiss it as an effective system because they cannot understand it from a theoretical point of view—they cannot see why it should work. Even its founder, Samuel

Hahnemann, could never explain full why it should work, only that it did. And he was right, as thousands who have been cured will testify. Similarly, with some mystical exercises, it is no good concentrating too much on the theory, what matters is the results. Later, gradually, possibly through deep meditation, you understand why, but you would probably never have been able to attain that level of meditation if you had not practised the mystical exercises in the first place.

As with the physical brain, so the psychic nature is divided into left and right poles, each with particular properties. Lengthy and complex tomes have been written about the characteristics of these different poles, but the most important thing to remember is that all powerful systems of breathing stress the need to isolate the breath individually into the left and right nostrils. You do this by blocking one side and independently drawing energies through the left or right nostril, thereby polarising the natural forces you draw into yourself. Just as energy is contained in the oxygen, so energy is contained in and around the physical body in an energy field, which is another term for the aura mentioned earlier. There is an undeniable need to demystify some yoga writings, and by looking at these phenomena in terms of natural energy you can start to do so.

While we should understand as much as possible of the theories, we must realise that this is a journey of discovery, that the real properties of these natural energies will only be revealed to us through direct experience. When you have charged yourself up with natural powers, you know that they exist because you can feel them. Here are some simple, safe, but effective breathing exercises you can use to magnetise yourself.

EXERCISE FIFTEEN: Left Nostril Breathing

According to ancient Sanskrit writings, the best time to breathe through the left nostril is during the daytime, between dawn and dusk. Obviously this does not mean that you should spend the whole day with your right nostril blocked! But it does mean that at a convenient time during the day you can potentise the natural energy flow within your mind and body by breathing solely through the left nostril for a few minutes. To do this, you simply place the thumb of your right hand along the right side of the nose and gently push it inwards so that you are no longer able to breathe through this nostril. You then inhale and exhale through the left nostril, trying to keep the in- and out-breaths as even as possible. You will draw to yourself one aspect of the energies which flow through the ethers of space, which could be referred to as the negative pole. This in no sense means negativity in terms of bad or negative in thinking, but refers purely to polarisation.

The negative pole is associated, among other things, with introspection, calmness, balance and spirituality. Sanskrit writings refer to it as the flow of the moon—the inward, receptive, mystical energies. You might think this is the exact opposite of what you want in the daytime when you are at your most active, but it is a mistake to look at it in that way. To the yogis who devised the systems of pranayama, it was a matter of becoming in harmony and attunement with nature and the cosmos and taking advantage of the best times to invoke whatever energies they required. These energies would then stay with them and be used at a time of their choosing. Of course they were primarily concerned with realising enlightened states of consciousness and would use their days for this purpose. To take advantage of the flow of negative pole energies they would be ready to commence their meditations at dusk.

Nowadays, in the hectic bustle of daily living and the demanding schedules most of us have, it is more valuable than ever to take a few minutes of the day to draw these calm, receptive energies to you by practising left nostril breathing. You can do this seated on a hard-backed chair with the shoulders relaxed and the spine straight, or in a suitable yoga asana if you know one. It can be done in a standing position, for example if you are outdoors and wish to practise this in a natural environment, which is the most potent place to do it. You can practise it every day or as regularly as possible and you will find that it brings a greater balance and mental clarity to your life, as well as giving you a gentle, but definite dynamism in your approach to all things.

EXERCISE SIXTEEN: Right Nostril Breathing

This exercise works in partnership with the previous one and should be performed equally regularly—it is important that you do not do one more than the other unless you have a specific reason for doing so, such as a nasal blockage in one nostril which you want to counterbalance by breathing through the other. There may come a stage when you start to understand the flow of natural energies so well that you know what you need at any specific time and therefore choose to draw on either the right or left nostril breathing for a particular time. But as a general rule, keep the two in balance as far as possible.

Right nostril breathing, according to ancient Sanskrit writings, is more potent at night-time, between dusk and dawn, which they call the flow of the sun. On the face of it, it should be the other way round, but the yogis were not referring to the times when the sun and moon are visible—they were then known as code names for the positive and negative poles of natural energy. The positive flow which you draw through the right nostril is more active, practical and creative. Some people swear they can be far more inspired at night, and this could be one reason for it. Of course it will depend on what flow you need, according to the balance of energies contained within your mind and body at any one time.

If you do left and right nostril breathing for a few minutes at the times suggested, you will magnetise yourself by drawing in this most prevalent and potent flow of energy, and this will stay with you to be used when appropriate. Please bear in mind that there are many systems of yoga breathing, which require you to do left, right or both nostril breathing at any time, and you should certainly do so. In order to gain higher states of consciousness you will need to use a system which incorporates all these things, but these two exercises I have given can also be done to attune yourself to the natural energy flows and thereby make you a more magnetic person with greater resources of mind power on which to draw.

EXERCISE SEVENTEEN: Holding the Breath

This exercise is the other essential ingredient in any system of breathing exercises, and one with amazing properties far beyond the apparently simple practice involved. It was referred to with great reverence in Sanskrit writings as *Kevala Kumbahka* and was said to be capable on its own of inducing elevated states of high consciousness and profound awareness of the oneness of all things. It must be practised gently, without force or strain, but if you have a weak heart it may be advisable not to do this exercise.

The intention of the yogis was to retain the breath for as long as possible, and there have been fantastic demonstrations of breath retention for 30 minutes or more. From the point of view of everyday living, this exercise will charge you up by drawing to you and holding within you natural magnetic energies which then charge up your mind and body. To paraphrase a well known advertisement, they reach the parts of you that other energies cannot reach!

Before holding the breath, you should practise rhythmic, harmonious breathing for a few moments. Then draw into yourself, slowly but definitely, as full a breath as possible. As you do so, imagine a white light entering the whole of your body and the energy field around your body. Hold the breath in for as long as you can without strain and then gently release it—do not let it go suddenly like a steam engine, but gradually in a controlled fashion. Continue the rhythmic breathing for a few moments and then do it again, and so on. Do this for a set number of times, but not too many—3, 5, 7 or 9 would be excellent, the odd numbers being more suitable according to numerological writings for this type of mystical exercise.

Colloquially people will often say, 'You'd better hold your breath,' or 'Don't bother to hold your breath,' when talking about a coming auspicious event or opportunity. As with so many sayings, there is a mystical root underlying this phrase. You hold your breath in order to magnetise yourself so that you can manifest this power later. If someone says, 'Don't hold your breath,' they mean (though they probably don't realise it) that this opportunity is not going to come so don't bother to magnetise yourself in preparation for it. Retention of the breath is a very powerful and symbolic act, which ultimately signifies the final return to complete superconscious awareness and, according to some belief systems, amalgamation with the divine. Whether you accept that or not, it will certainly magnetise you with natural energies if practised regularly, but without any force.

ENERGY SOURCES

There are other ways of charging yourself up with natural energies—by visiting places which contain them in a potent way. Places of pilgrimage are an obvious example of this. Many will attest to the healing miracles they have experienced at Lourdes in France—a site of Roman Catholic pilgrimage. This is not only because of the place itself: the countless thousands who have visited it over the years have given power to it through their faith, and belief translated into mind energy has potentised the place. Others visit ancient sites such as Stonehenge in Wiltshire and the Pyramids of Giza in Egypt and attest to the great powers they experience there. Again, the energy associated with these places has been potentised by the many who visited over the centuries.

There is another factor at work, especially in the pyramids—namely Shape Power. The pyramid shape, among others, has been shown to have powerful effects of its own by drawing together natural energies in a certain way. A central data pool for pyramid research was established in Washington by Mankind Research Unlimited in 1973. Dr Boris Vern, its director, conducted pilot experiments using plastic pyramids ten inches high. He found that raw eggs placed under the pyramids hardened and dried in less than three weeks. Moulds placed on those eggs would not grow, whereas eggs not placed under pyramids remained moist and acted as receptive media to enhance mould growth. Others found that small pyramids could be used to sharpen razor blades placed under them and this principle was successfully marketed commercially. The only reason for these results could have been the shape power of the pyramid, which was undoubtedly intended by the ancient Egyptians for much higher purposes than this.

The Cross is another shape which has certain inherent powers quite apart from the religious connotations of Christianity which it predates. The shape of the building you live in will affect your mood, because of the vibrations it draws to the place. For example, a dome has long been regarded as a shape conducive to worship, and not only in the East, for there are certain examples in the West such as St Paul's in the City of London and St Peter's in Rome.

There are also modern places of pilgrimage visited by members and sympathisers of The Aetherius Society, who regard nineteen mountains in the world as having been charged with special cosmic powers since 1958. Because these are relatively recent, some of them have not yet been visited very frequently, although they have all been climbed—some hundreds of times. You can tell that the natural energies there, which can be experienced, are not purely the result of the faith and belief of the pilgrims, but of a definite, tangible power. Sceptics have been amazed at the experiences they have had on these mountains.

As well as specific places of pilgrimage, it is possible to affect environments, by giving power to certain parts of buildings for specific purposes. A system known as Feng Shui uses this concept as part of its system. One expert practitioner found it so effective that at times she had to temper its results. She was involved in public relations and placed a large, beautiful plant in the part of the room she associated with fame. She found that this drew so many calls to her office from journalists that she could not cope with them all. She placed a rubbish bin by the plant and they immediately stopped. This is certainly an example of using mind energies with extraordinary results.

An area of growing popularity is crystal healing, again because it is believed that you can magnetise yourself in various ways by using quartz crystals. They are said to be particularly susceptible to the moon, which stimulates the energy field of quartz crystal. When it is drawn closer by the gravitational pull of the Earth—as at the time of a full moon—its close proximity stimulates all magnetic fields. The inbuilt electromagnetic properties of the crystal are intensified during such periods and emit potent forces which, according to some, can be felt as a severe pressure on the crown of the head.

Crystal healing utilises the ability of quartz to draw natural energies to you, so that it can be drawn on when you choose. However, it is a very experimental field and much still has to be learnt about storing and releasing magnetic energy from quartz crystal. What definitely has been proved by many practitioners is that crystals are conducive to magnetic energies and can have an effect on the natural vibrations of an environment.

From studying these phenomena you start to realise that the whole of life can virtually become a ritual, invoking and drawing to you the natural energies you require. If certain clothes have specific meanings for you and you only wear them for that purpose, they will gain a power for you. If, for example, you have clothes specifically reserved for mind and supermind exercises, they will attract these energies to them. Then, when you wear them, it will be that much easier to slip automatically into the frame of mind you want to be in when doing these practices; they will be imbued with the right energies.

This vast sea of natural energy that we all live in is just waiting to be tapped. None of us use it as fully as we could. It is something you can only really discover by practice. When you start to become aware of the natural flows of energy in which we all exist, and draw it to you more often, you will feel the difference. You will become more magnetic, and then you will be able to radiate powers to others as well as yourself, far more than you have ever done before.

11

Radiating Power to Others

*

As well as controlling the effect that energy has upon us, it is very important to predetermine the energy we radiate through ourselves, as far as we can. This is especially true when you start to realise that, as the Lord Buddha said, 'To every action there is an equal and opposite reaction'. In other words, whatever energy we relay will tend to bring the same type of energy back to us.

GIVING AND RECEIVING

We can see this simply in our everyday lives. If a person radiates aggression towards another person, he nearly always receives aggression back. Nowhere is this more commonly seen than driving on the road. If one driver swears at another he is very likely to receive an oath back, whereas a courteous driver is more likely to receive a wave as an expression of appreciation or, if you like, a good vibration. Whatever vibrations you relay into the sea of energy around you, you tend to receive back into yourself.

The Hindus referred to this process as the Law of Karma. Unfortunately, too many people associate purely negative connotations with Karma. When someone refers to 'getting

Karma' he normally means something bad. John Lennon's song 'Instant Karma', while very revolutionary in its day, epitomises this negative approach, portraying it as some avenging force. The Sword of Damocles concept of Divine Law is not really helpful in understanding and manipulating what is really a very natural process. If you put out negative energy into the sea of mind, you will draw negative energy back to yourself, but if you put out positive energy you will get this back and create a self-generating powerstation of ever-increasing energy to draw upon.

The New Testament parable of the talents is all about this—not just about investing money, though even that is a form of energy. You need to put all energy to work for you and then it will potentise itself and accumulate more and more. You do this by radiating it outwards, not trying to hoard it for yourself. It sounds corny, but if you smile genuinely you send out a positive beam of energy in the direction of the person you smile at. He then responds at a mental level and you empower yourself as well as him. If you look gloomy, you drain yourself and you receive nothing back in response. In terms of mind energy, it is a regressive cycle of energy inter-action instead of an accumulative one.

Dr George King expresses the function of the mind as being rather like a pincushion. When you put out a thought you push a pin into the cushion. The pin in turn leaves a hole in the cushion which makes it that much easier for the same pin (the same thought) to return into that position. In other words, the thought processes of the brain are habitual and you tend to attract what you are used to attracting to you. The same applies to your relationships with others: if you treat another person very badly he will not respond warmly to you. It is also true of our relationship with the environment. If we continue to pollute the environment, which is a result of an unthinking approach on our part, the environment will deteriorate and eventually will respond with all sorts of cataclysmic results.

On the positive side, if you recognise the abilities of others (which, by the way, is a very different thing from flattering them), this will bring in return an appreciation of your own abilities. If the whole of society were based upon a network of recognition of each other's abilities, rather than a competitive, destructive, negative approach among the peoples of the world, then society as a whole would flourish.

LOVE ENERGY

All this is really an expression of the timeless energy called Love. You do not have to be a saint to radiate love, but you do have to work at it, it does not always come naturally. In my view, there is far too much emphasis nowadays on personal morality and not nearly enough on global morality. Of course, we should all strive to fulfil the highest ideals of our chosen moral, ethical or religious codes in our private lives. If we cannot do this we shall be unable to sustain a high degree of morality in our public concerns. But it is unrealistic to suggest that a person's private behaviour is more important than his global concerns—it is the other way round.

The New Age movement is understandably confusing to many people, because of the many different views expressed, including some which really do not belong in it at all. The emphasis in the New Age will not be primarily upon personal development or private relationships and morality, but upon global concerns, breaking down the barriers between peoples, cultures and religions; the removal of class consciousness and racial discrimination; the establishment of the role of women as a force equally important to the betterment of the world as that of men. Above all, the New Age will be about radiating love to all people. It will not be about loving just one's own family, which, after all, is very easy to do. It is far more difficult to radiate love to those you have never met, to those who are probably in far greater need than your own close relatives and friends.

This radiation of love has to be expressed on many levels. Some would say that it is not a purely mental thing and they would be right. Mind in its fullest sense goes beyond the brain and intellect and extends to the whole of our being. Mystical teaching from both East and West refers to the existence of *chakras* or psychic centres in the human aura. There are many of these, but there are seven major ones: base of the spine centre; sex centre; solar plexus centre; heart centre; throat centre; Christ centre (or third eye) between the eyebrows; and the crown centre, above the top of the head. These are all located in the aura which is the energy body surrounding the physical body. They are all centres of mind energy which affect the expression of our thoughts and feelings.

Whether or not you accept concepts like this, you do start to realise that mind is a form of energy which envelops the whole of your being. By radiating love for all life you start to bring a balance to the function of the whole of your being and a purification to the channels through which mind energy flows.

So how do you learn to develop this feeling of love for others? The following exercise will be very valuable for this purpose:

EXERCISE EIGHTEEN:
Sending Love Energy to an Individual

When you are in the presence of a person who is either irritating to you or in need of help, you can go one step farther than the self-protection practice (p. 131). This time you don't just draw the white light into you when you breathe in, but on the out-breath you radiate it out again. On the in-breath you start to draw into the whole of your being a white light filling you and surrounding you and protecting you from unwanted vibrations. On the out-breath you start to radiate this white light to the other person and above all try to feel a certain love for him or her. This love should not be emotional or sentimental. It should certainly not be dishonest and you should not pretend that a person is someone he is not in order to love him more easily. It should be a kind of impersonal love for all life, a protective, preservative, healing love that wishes the very best for that person, and no more than that. You are visualising this light travelling from you to him and you are sending him love energy. You should not attempt to change his mind or get him to do what you feel he should do, for this is interfering with his free will, which is negative magic and will rebound on you. Just send him your love.

In the previous chapter I referred to the universal life forces pervading all creation. Love is the energy that will temper and condition those forces, the vibration that will flow with them in a cycle of thought waves. All energy travels in waves or cycles and thought is no exception to this.

If you see thought as just another form of energy, you are in a very good position to start to control it. Those who see their thoughts and feelings as being beyond their control are quite wrong. How improved their lives would be if they could recognise that we are the masters of our minds. As we have seen, one of the ways to start to gain control over your thoughts and feelings is the practice of affirmation. You should repeat a statement verbally, either silently or aloud to yourself, which is in every way positive and affirms the result you wish to attain. The famous affirmation I referred to earlier, 'Every day in every way I am getting better and better', which has worked for so many people, is an assertion made by the conscious mind which is then registered by the subconscious mind which in turn causes it to happen.

Alcoholics who are in recovery all agree on one thing: there came a point in their lives when they decided in their heart of hearts to change. Sometimes they felt guilty for the harm they were doing to others; sometimes they really wanted to re-establish their self-pride; sometimes it was just severe physical and mental anguish. But whatever it was, at some point they made a decision, a determination that they would overcome this weakness. From that moment they planted a thought in their brain which gave their subconscious mind the opportunity to co-operate with it; the wheels, if you like, were set in motion for recovery. Of course, tremendous efforts had to be made along the way, but as soon as that determination was made, it became possible.

This principle remains true in all things. I believe that those of us who look in the mirror and judge the reflection we see by the lesson of love as demonstrated, say, by Jesus Christ, the Lord Buddha, Gandhi, Schweitzer or some other great figure, will be honest enough to admit that we fall considerably short. This is nothing to be unduly ashamed of, but it is something we can change if we wish. The following is an affirmation you can use to enhance love in your life.

EXERCISE NINETEEN: Affirmation for Love

Repeat to yourself with great feeling, either aloud or quietly, the following words: 'I will radiate the energy of love to all life.' In an affirmation, it is vitally important to make a determination for the future and not to pretend that one has already achieved something. For example, you should not say: 'I always radiate love,' because this would not be true, but you can say, 'I will radiate love' because that is a determination about the present and future. Some prefer to say it aloud and some prefer to say it silently, inside their minds. If you are in doubt I would recommend in the early stages that you say it aloud, because most people find it is easier to concentrate on the spoken word. You may, however, find yourself in conditions where you cannot say it aloud and then you can certainly say it quietly to yourself.

Practise this exercise for at least several minutes. You can do it in most places, but obviously you should not attempt it if you are driving a car or are engaged on some other demanding task which requires your concentration. Gradually, by doing this practice, you will enhance your natural radiation of love energy.

You can decide to use the energy of love more fully in your life, and if you do you will help to start a trend, sowing seeds which will blossom later. Negative thinking, which radiates a negative vibration, sooner or later returns to you. It is regressive and eventually ends in metaphorical tears. But positive energy, which love is, sows the seeds of growth. From them other seeds form and so it goes on, generating itself with the interaction of others who receive this energy from you, knowingly or unknowingly, and also feel inspired to radiate love. After all, we all like love. It is beautiful, it is attractive, we know in our heart of hearts that it is right. When you see people in a hostile environment, such as a street gang, intent on fighting another street gang, although there is maybe a bravado fuelled by egoism and hatred, they are not really happy. But when you see people living in harmony and radiating love they are at peace, enjoying themselves. Love is the natural way.

Here is an exercise you can use to enhance the energy of love in your life and therefore in the lives of others as well. If you like you can use it after the Affirmation for Love Exercise—it will follow on perfectly.

EXERCISE TWENTY:
Sending Love Energy to the World

Sit in a comfortable position in the usual way. Do not lie down on your back for this, because you want to avoid drowsiness. Practise a few deep breaths in order to alert your mind, and then select a situation which does not intimately involve you in any way. It should be a situation of need, such as a war zone, an earthquake zone, a hospital or a peace negotiation. It may be more local than this, but it should not be any situation in which you have a direct emotional involvement through relatives or friends, particularly in the early stages of practice.

When you think of this situation, do not visualise any of the suffering involved in your mind; just think about the situation in general, in a purely abstract way. You do not want to give power in your thoughts to any negative images, but should just identify the situation mentally. The more impersonal you can be about this practice the better, because then you will learn to radiate love at will.

Having identified your situation, start to radiate love to it in the following way. Imagine the geographical location—a city where a peace negotiation is going on, perhaps, or even a building in that city. If it is a war zone you may be able to imagine it on a map. Now imagine the location being filled with white light, being illuminated and lifted upwards, and try to feel in your heart a true love, a true concern, a true compassion for all the people involved in that situation. Do not try to do this for too long, but just for a few minutes, and then stop. And when you stop completely detach. Do not dwell on it, let it go.

This exercise will do two things for you. Firstly, it will start to teach you to radiate love at will. Secondly, it will bring about a positive change to the sea of mind which will reflect on that situation. After all, you have introduced into the mind belt, which is the mind substance of the world, a ray of light and this ray of light must have an effect. Just as anger must have an effect on the mind belt of the world, so love, even more surely, has a definite effect. The exercise can only do good.

If in the middle of the exercise you find your mind wandering from the subject, bring it back; then you will be starting to gain control of the radiation of your love energy. Always bring it back to the focus of concentration of the exercise and demonstrate to your subconscious mind that you are now determining the direction of the energy of mind.

RADIATING ENERGY

One thing is certain: there is great power to the radiation of thought, and especially of love energy. When you concentrate your mind upon a specific positive focus, accompanying it with true feeling, you can metaphorically move mountains. You can certainly bring a change to your environment and great benefit to others as well as yourself. You will find that the radiating of energies is greatly appreciated by animals, who often respond to it immediately. It also has a powerful effect on plants. Their growth patterns are better when positive energy is sent to them.

By radiating natural energies outwards, you will not only alter atmosphere for the good and lighten up the lives of others, you will introduce something else into your life. As well as greater personal power, you will also have a stronger sense of purpose and direction than you had before. If this motivating force is channelled correctly, you will then be able to open the door to supermind as never before.

12

The Key to Self-Motivation

*

Surveys have shown that people who include somewhere in their lives philanthropic or humanitarian activities, for no personal reward, are far more likely to be happy and fulfilled than those who do not. Depression is much more common among those who lead a purely selfish existence than among those who take part in altruistic activities. The reason for this is obvious. There is nothing more satisfying than the feeling that you have achieved something worthwhile, for the good of others. Selfish indulgence can be very pleasant in the short term, but it leads you on to want more and more for yourself. Deeds of valour, beneficence and charity have a lasting reward.

All this may sound like pious platitudes, but it is essential to a full understanding of the true motivations behind your mind impulses. After all, it is motivation that is going to be the key to manifesting the full potential of your mind. There is an urge to achieve in all people, which can manifest in many different areas—business, family life, sporting activities, social life or humanitarian activities. We have to choose where we wish to put our energies and then become motivated about it.

A PURPOSE FOR LIVING

In business there is a satisfaction that comes from a job well done. You know that you have provided a service and this gives you a feeling of worth and value which helps to give a greater sense of purpose to your life. There are, of course, those who are purely motivated to make money and they are not very interested how they do it. Such people, though, will not find the same peace of mind that comes from service to others. The desire for acquisition is never appeased.

Many people devote their giving natures to their family. Not only parents but brothers, sisters, children and other relatives can spend a tremendous amount of time and energy trying to help members of their family in one way or another. It is certainly important to do this, but it is a mistake to think that this is where your responsibilities end. The inner urge to serve goes beyond the family community. We are more aware today of world conditions and with that awareness goes an increased sense of responsibility for the suffering of others whether they be relatives of ours, fellow countrymen or not. This is a positive development and one that was prophesied by many to take place as the new millennium dawns: a time of greater global consciousness and a recognition that we are interlinked with all people, whether they are on the other side of the world or in the house next door.

This consciousness of our relationship with others is not just altruism. Once you realise that a mind belt of energies exists around the planet, you realise that we are all affected by one another. Perhaps the most stressful aspect of modern living is the awareness of the dangers which affect us all. The existence of potentially lethal atomic weaponry is not an isolated political matter between world leaders, it affects us all directly. Terrorism is not just something we hear about, it is an arbitrary force of evil which could be inflicted upon anyone. And so on. Hence co-operating with a force for good in the world is not just worthy, it is a key to self-motivation as well.

How many people watch the news on television in the evening and feel a sense of desolation and uselessness? Yet responses to help the suffering victims of war-torn areas, of hurricanes, earthquakes and floods, are increasing in the world. By doing something about it, people satisfy a troubled conscience; they follow a natural innate urge, and although it does not remove their concern, it gives them a greater peace of mind.

The old quest for peace without concern for others is bound to be limited in its permanence. Despite the fact that many who advocate meditation away from humanity and without concern for others will tell you that by doing this you help all people indirectly, today that is not enough. People need to serve directly; they need to participate in the world process and by doing so they will start to unlock their inner potential. You experience a greater degree of inspiration, inner satisfaction and self-worth through service to others.

Of course, you always need to work on self-improvement as well if you wish to attain a higher level of mental power. The urge for personal attainment that you see, for example, in outstanding athletes, is marvellous to behold. Their relentless drive for excellence is commendable. No doubt, the fact that they bring pleasure to millions who watch them, and a degree of hope about human potential, all adds to the satisfaction they get from their career. Increasingly, of late, there is the added motivation of large sums of money and arguably this has done much to lower the tone of sporting activities. An increased amount of violence and aggressive competitiveness has come with the excessive amounts of money changing hands. This did not happen so much when sport was done more for its own sake and for the sake of those who watched.

In analysing the use of mind power throughout your life,

whether it be enhancing memory, improved concentration or the increased ability to tap into higher aspects of mind, your motivation will be absolutely crucial. You will find that the more altruistic your motivation, the more accessible your inspirational and intuitive faculties will become as they respond better to this approach.

FINDING YOUR DESTINY

The great Chinese sage Lao Tzu said, 'Returning to one's destiny is known as the constant. Knowledge of the constant is known as discernment.' In other words, the key to successful living is to recognise your true destiny, and if you are capable of doing this you will have the faculty of insight and wisdom. It is not so much a question of how important a person's life work is, it is whether they are fulfilling it that counts. You can find people in positions of great prominence who are not really fulfilled by their status in life. It may be that they had a destiny to include in their lives other areas of personal attainment and service. On the other hand, there are those who lack ambition and never achieve the sort of levels of which they are capable. Many content themselves with a so-called 'ordinary life' which really does not satisfy them. It is not a question of what you do, but of whether you are fulfilling yourself. Sometimes you have a calling which you know is for you. Follow it. Only then will your full mental potential be awakened. Until then there will be a certain subconscious frustration or an inner voice telling you that things are wrong and you do not really know why.

Finding your destiny is not necessarily a complex thing, it is just a question of self-examination. Most people know inside what they are cut out for, what their real drives are—the ones that count—but whatever they are, they will not work fully if they are completely selfish. There is a natural soul urge, if you like, in all people to contribute something. You can see this even in reformed criminals who, when they do change, will tell you that for the first time they feel a sense of self-worth and value. This too is part of the expression of the mind.

Ordinary people do not really exist—we are all extraordinary in one way or another. Politicians like to praise the 'man in the street' because they depend on such a person for their votes. They like to praise so-called 'ordinary values' because they feel that this flattery will reward them at the next election. These so-called ordinary people, on the other hand, do not hold a high opinion of politicians, as countless opinion polls tell us. Perhaps it is because politicians appeal to the wrong qualities in us. Perhaps people do not wish to be encouraged to lead an 'ordinary life', but wish to be called upon for greater things. One of the most popular politicians in the history of Great Britain was Sir Winston Churchill who constantly called on people to bring out the greatness in their lives, not to continue in mundane ordinariness—to rise to the occasion.

This urge to make a mark on world events is symptomatic of that urge to rise above ordinary values into something greater, something more lasting for the world as a whole. This part of the mind is very much neglected. Psychologists often refer to basic urges such as sexual desire, but how often do you hear them talking about altruistic urges which can also be buried unless they are developed and brought out? When you start to give service to others in your own chosen way, you will find a fulfilment second to none, and this in turn will help you use your latent mental powers.

FOCUS ON GREATNESS

One way of really developing the altruistic side of your nature, or indeed any ability you wish to develop, is to concentrate your attention upon a favourite hero or heroine. For example, most of us admire people like Dr Albert Schweitzer, Mother Theresa of Calcutta and other saintly persons who have devoted their lives in the service of their fellow human beings. We could go one step farther and mention names like Jesus Christ, the Lord Buddha, Shri Krishna and other spiritual giants. By focusing on such personages we can start to emulate some of their great characteristics. The following contemplation exercise will help you to do this.

EXERCISE TWENTY-ONE:
Contemplation on Greatness

Sit down and practise a few deep, rhythmic breaths. Before doing this exercise, you will have selected your chosen focus of contemplation. Make sure it is a person of greatness. It should not just be a person who has achieved great things, but someone who has exhibited in his or her life qualities of compassion, self-sacrifice, kindness, goodness, determination and so on.

Start the exercise by thinking about this person by name, and all the great things you know about him. In order to get value from the exercise, do not think about any negative factors at all, just the good ones. If your chosen person is great enough, you should get a feeling which starts to fill you and invigorate you. The principle, after all, is that if you are in the company of people they will affect your behaviour. In this case you are mentally putting yourself in tune with characteristics of greatness and these vibrations, through your contemplation, will come into you so that you should feel changed by them.

Do this gently, without any force, and it can be extremely rewarding for you. Do not, at any stage, try to imagine the person in your presence or put any kind of demand upon him whatsoever. Nor should you start to identify yourself with him or to create in your mind any kind of relationship with him. You are purely first thinking about and then contemplating the great achievements of the person in question, so that these characteristics and the energy associated with them will start to come back to you. It would be safest to perform this practice on someone who is not physically alive.

Even if all your facts are not completely correct, nevertheless, it is the image which is important, rather than the individual himself. Provided we place no demands upon that person in our thoughts, the energies associated with him can only be of benefit to us.

Some people, right from childhood, have always wanted to help others in one way or another. Others really do not seem to care at all. It is not a question of being 'do-gooders', but of finding mental fulfilment and contributing to the whole. After all, we are all cells in one interrelated whole which is the human race. We also have a responsibility for the animal kingdom, plant life and the very Earth on which we live. Already an awareness is growing of these responsibilities and you will find that the most motivated people in the world are those who have a cause. It is unusual in a book on the mind to mention things like this, since most of them are written from a purely self-centred point of view: How can I enhance my life? How can I improve my mind? How can I find peace? and so on. I think writers underestimate the innate desire of people to make a difference. Yes, certainly we all want to find more peace, more satisfaction, more fulfilment, and there is nothing wrong with that, but we also want to contribute.

SPIRITUAL VALUES

The 1960s, which are now ridiculed and berated, nevertheless brought a permanent change to world consciousness. Not the drugs, the amorality and the self-indulgence—that aspect has been exposed as the hypocrisy of the decade: 'When they said love, they really meant sex; when they said peace, they really meant drugs.' But there was also an element of lasting value— the willingness to turn away from purely material ideals to try to find something more rewarding on a higher level of consciousness. Of course the total lack of discipline destroyed it. The values soon disappeared when the hard realities of material existence came to the fore.

This happens so often, not just to cultural eras, but to individuals as well. They start out in life highly motivated and lose their motivation in the mists of material responsibilities and family duty. If this has happened to you, step back from it all and make the change. You cannot bypass material responsibilities, but you can absorb them. You can make them just a part of your life's purpose instead of being so swamped by them that you haven't got time to think whether there is a purpose or not. To do this you have to detach from your own problems and concentrate on the problems of others. Not only does this give you a much better perspective on your own life, but it releases a suppressed part of your nature, a part that really wants to soar beyond mundanity into the superconscious part of your being, the supermind.

It is amazing how resilient we all are. I have seen middle-aged and elderly people completely change their perspective on life, to do what the Americans call 'reprioritise'. It is possible to cast off the shackles of limitation while accepting the role convention has carved out for you. So many people feel trapped or, worse, disillusioned. They think that all the high ideals of their youth were illusory, fantasy, and they give up on them and opt for so-called normality. What they actually then become is a slave to the mind belt, not its manipulator.

SOCIAL CONDITIONING

It is for you to determine your destiny—you do not have to become the product of a mass thought form. In the general consciousness of any social group in any culture, there is a very definite concept of how people are expected to behave, and yet there are enormous differences between some of these social behaviour systems. This proves that socially acceptable behaviour is not really normal at all—if it was, the criteria of all groups would be the same. One culture may be purely monogamous, while another regards it as the height of good manners to practise wife swapping; one culture believes you should fight to the death for your honour, another that you should forgive and spare life at all costs, and so on. There is no norm, only different standards of behaviour determined by mind patterns built up over cultural groupings—you could call it group consciousness.

The key to self-motivation is not to be ruled by this, but to contribute to it—to accept the values which are obviously worthwhile, and help to change those which are not. We can see just how limiting mental conditioning can be by looking at the inspired geniuses of history. They have virtually all broken free in one way or another from accepted thinking and made a radical change to science, the arts, religion or some other field. In many cases they have been ridiculed, reviled, or worse. Galileo is a prime example of someone who was forced to recant because his ideas, correct though they proved to be, did not fit with the scientific and religious dogmas of the day.

Modern culture is no exception. When you are promoting a subject like natural healing, ESP or UFOs, as I have done internationally for many years, you come up directly against an inbuilt prejudice from many people. In some cases I would say that this prejudice is so deep it is rooted in the subconscious. Some people who have absorbed a certain strand of thinking react against you instinctively and often illogically. One release for this type of subconscious conditioning is to laugh—the reaction of a child to something he does not understand.

I am not saying for a moment that I expect everyone to agree with my views on healing, ESP or UFOs—why should they? But while disagreement and healthy debate are useful and appropriate ways of dealing with an important issue, resorting to mockery as a way of not even having to consider something is not. I believe, for example, that Jesus Christ came from another planet. Some find that shocking at first, but only because they have been raised in a culture which has been imbued for centuries with the concept of Jesus as the one and only Son of God. And yet if you examine the two concepts, my belief is far less radical from a theological point of view. If a completely neutral person who had never heard of Jesus or the Bible was presented with these two possible explanations, he would have to admit that the idea of the Star of Bethlehem being a spacecraft and bringing to Earth an exceptional, god-like being called Jesus is far more likely than the fact that the Creator of the entire Universe decided once in the history of mankind to incarnate in one part of the world only and live there for thirty-three years.

I say this not to open up a theological debate, because I respect all views and many readers will not believe either of these two concepts. I am purely illustrating the power of the mind belt to distort our perspective of things and the need to find the key to your own motivation, regardless of what may or may not be expected of you by others. Charles Dickens is a classic example of someone who did this. He chose subjects for his novels which were not conventionally or socially acceptable—poverty, child abuse, cruelty, miserliness and so on. Hardly the stuff of a Jane Austen novel. So good was his writing that not only the novels, but the subjects they dealt with, became popular. No one can say how much he altered the consciousness of Victorian England to start to deal with philanthropic and humanitarian issues; my own view is that the influence of Dickens on the mind belt, particularly in relation to child welfare, is still with us today.

MAKING A MARK

But Dickens is a good example of something else, too. He needed this focus for his genius to awaken the outstanding forces of inspiration within him. For him, it was not enough just to write about relationships between members of the landed classes; in order to be fired up he needed to feel he was making an important contribution to the human condition. This has been true of many other artistic geniuses through history. They have not taken the easy way. They have needed to find a higher purpose for their art, one which they believed to be important to the world. This sense of higher purpose has been a key to their self-motivation.

A contribution made to others leaves its mark—a certain permanence. One of the quests of all the Zen teachers, Yoga masters and practitioners of meditation was to find a state of permanence. They said that even if you want happiness, you cannot successfully make it your goal because it is a fleeting thing, it comes and it goes. But if you seek out a state of permanence, you will find with it an inherent joy and, if you go far enough, bliss. Those feelings of inner contentment will not come if you have not in some way given service to others, because there is a part of you that needs this, just as surely as you need to eat, drink, exercise and perform all the other functions of life. You can see it in working people. Those who work hard, although the pay is no better for this, radiate a sense of satisfaction and vibrancy which is missing in those who do the minimum. Laziness breeds laziness, giving breeds giving and the more you give the more you will be able to receive. Those who are willing to help their fellow human beings in one way or another—and there are numerous ways of doing it—are more likely to awaken their inner powers and thereby attain the goals they seek.

13

Attain Your Highest Goals

*

Experiments performed by scientists have shown that, in addition to the brain, there is a part of our being which operates fractions of a second before the brain is activated. Sensitive meters attached to subjects showed that before the impulse of the brain instructed a part of the body to operate, something else had taken place within the psyche of the individual. Some took this to indicate the existence of a soul, others that there is another part of a person's nature which is not yet understood. But whatever your interpretation of this, it does point to the existence of a faculty of will quite independent from the brain itself.

WILL-POWER

No matter what you do in life, no matter what your goal is or what you hope to achieve, you will not do it if you do not have the will to succeed. It is will, at the end of the day, which sees us through. When a mountaineer is struggling to make his final steps towards the summit, it is sheer will-power that leads him on—not reasoned argument or even some emotional desire to achieve his goal, but the same instinctive faculty that we all possess.

Earlier in the book I referred to Dr Shastri's concept of suspending the lower will. By this he meant suspending our desires if they are not in tune with what we feel or believe to be right for us and for others—in other words, observing our inner thoughts and making a choice as to how we will act and whether or not we will follow the promptings of our mind. It is through will that this choice is made: the higher will suspends the lower will.

There are some things we do in life which we can never really explain. In emergencies people have been able to muster the tremendous physical strength needed to open doors that had been blocked during an earthquake, using a force which should have been beyond them. People who have never swum have been able to swim when they should have drowned, without understanding how they did it. One could cite many examples of superhuman feats in crisis situations. It is a well-known fact that in time of war and trouble, many people will rise to an occasion, who would not normally do so. What is it that enables them to act in a way that is out of character, even out of their normal mind pattern? It is sheer will.

Most of us are experts at making excuses, not only to others but to ourselves. It becomes such a habit that we do it almost instinctively. Not only is this dishonest to others, but most of all we damage ourselves because we are undermining our own will-power. We are denying our weaknesses and therefore denying ourselves the opportunity to overcome them. Positive thinking will do many things for us, but the most important thing it will do is develop our will-power.

No matter where you set your sights, will-power will lead you to success. It is a very good affirmation to say to yourself, 'I will succeed in achieving this or that.' In any endeavour, especially an important one, there are times when you lose heart and feel that the tide is set against you. Sometimes you have no reason or desire to go on with a particular course of action, but somehow you do; something inside you drives you on. That is the part of you that you need the most.

The will is a wonderful part of our nature which needs to be cultivated and nurtured in every possible way. There is tremendous truth in the saying that success breeds success, but why does it do so? Simply because it gives you the ability to believe in your own success. When you can see an achievement, you believe that you can do it again. The first time you practise spiritual healing successfully on another person, you do more for your healing ability than all the faith you might have needed to get started, because now you know from first-hand experience that you can do it. The first time you ride a bike without falling off, you feed your will-power because you are giving yourself a signal that you can do it. Will is all about saying 'I can' and rejecting 'I can't'.

All the great achievers in history have been people of will and sheer determination. They have met obstacles on the way and continued despite them; no one has been able to put them off. When you follow a belief system that is unconventional, you may feel that there is something wrong with you. But if you look at the mess the world is in, you realise that it results from the thinking of the majority of people on Earth, either directly or indirectly, and you think, who wants to be conventional? The next time you find yourself making an excuse, either verbally or in your own mind, for something you have or have not done, stop yourself. Ask yourself what the real truth of the situation is, and if you have done something wrong, admit it—at least to yourself. Then you have the basis to determine to change and this is where your will-power is activated. If you are not honest with yourself you cannot change. Get rid of that habit of making excuses for inactivity, for not being successful and not achieving your goals. Cast them aside. They are undermining influences—go for the will to succeed.

A truly positive person will always reinforce the positive in others. It is the person who is insecure about himself who feels the need to be competitive and put other people down. Where you recognise talent, achievement and success, praise it. You will find if you do this that a certain magic will come into your life and will attract back to you the very things you praised and recognised. This will give power to your inner self and the determination to achieve your own goals.

SETTING GOALS

It is very important to decide exactly what your goals are, and you must be practical about this. I have met numerous people who had good, worthwhile goals which were completely unrealistic. They could not possibly achieve them, at least in the short term, so they were bound to be disappointed. Set yourself a realistic goal which you can achieve and then set out to accomplish it. By all means have a long-term plan for the future, but go step by step, and as you achieve each step along the way you will reinforce your will to go on to the next one. For example, if your goal is to be a surgeon and you have the capability to do so, set out to achieve this. First you will have to get into the right medical school, and having done this you must pass the necessary exams. After this you will have to go through a period of training in hospitals, and so on. You will need to concentrate on each stage as you tackle it, always with your sights on the final goal of becoming a surgeon.

This will to succeed is not always a good thing, of course. Both Hitler and Napoleon had tremendous will-power. Swami Sivananda believed that Napoleon was a person who had developed phenomenal mental powers of concentration in a former incarnation but had fallen from the path. I am not advocating the sort of selfish will-power that rides roughshod over others in order to achieve what you want. This will not lead to the kind of success I am talking about. Such people very often end up lonely and unfulfilled, despite their apparent success.

The sort of success I mean is success in the journey of life. Evolution is measured in experience, which is itself governed by realisation on a mental and physical level. There are remarkable examples of people who have achieved great success despite all odds. Gandhi, to name just one, did the unthinkable by leading India to independence without encouraging any form of violence. Madame Blavatsky, a Russian woman living in Victorian England, managed to write some of the most controversial metaphysical books that had ever been published and sold thousands of copies to serious readers. Even today, many years after her death, she still receives vilification of every kind. She has been accused of being a fraud by people who have only hearsay to go on. She had to put up with every kind of bigotry and yet she continued to spread her message of contact with Ascended Masters from secret retreats around the Earth, in the midst of a social climate conditioned by narrow-minded prejudice.

Nowadays, because of the advances of science, Western society has become far more materially comfortable for most of us than it used to be. Many people now enjoy ample nourishment, luxury and entertainment. But too much comfort can undermine your will-power. That is why some people feel the need, despite a luxurious lifestyle, to take on a pursuit which includes the excitement of a physical challenge such as mountaineering, skiing or cross-country running. There is a part of us which is crying out to conquer any obstacles in our way, and this needs to be nurtured, just like any other important quality.

The need for bravery is particularly important at the present time. It is unfortunate that most people wait for an emergency to arise before bringing out this noble part of their nature, but then they will react in the most superb manner. In car accidents, fires, earthquakes, there are countless tales of self-sacrificing actions by human beings whose spirit of courage and determination rose to the occasion when they witnessed others in distress. This spirit needs to be fed. It is a rare individual who will set himself a goal in life when there is no emergency in his immediate environment pressuring him to do so. There are those who join the Red Cross and travel to dangerous areas to help the needy, who work in emergency casualty departments in hospitals, who join police forces in dangerous cities and take their lives in their hands every night. They are the rare individuals who are rising to face a real challenge. Those people who set out to speak openly and more importantly live their beliefs despite ridicule, scepticism and the conditioning which comes from orthodox religious and scientific dogma, also require courage and determination. The measure of their success will be their bravery and will-power.

There is an old saying that God helps those who help themselves. Whether you believe in God or have some other name for what is meant by God, the principle is certainly true. If you make the effort to improve your life and help others, you start to receive some force or energy to give you the strength and determination to go on. This is a force which we can tap within ourselves by using will-power in our lives.

Will-power is very closely related to self-confidence; the two will nourish each other within us. It is not enough just to have a positive thought or idea: in order to realise it you have to put it into active manifestation through practical expression and this is where your will-power starts to grow within you and blossom. Some people who speak about the power of the mind dwell too much on the world of ideas and not enough on the world of physical action. Mind power is not an escape from life but a way to enhance and reinforce life in order to make it a more successful process and a more fulfilling experience in every way.

Discipline is out of vogue nowadays, and personal

expression is in. But you can have both, indeed you cannot successfully have one without the other. We all need discipline in one way or another if we are going to achieve anything. There is a part of us that enjoys self-discipline and gets a sense of personal satisfaction from it. In some ways it is like a bitter but health-giving medicine. The first taste of it may be unpleasant, but as it is absorbed by your physiological system you feel this great harmony and well-being pervade you. So it is with discipline when applied to a worthwhile goal.

It is very important when developing will-power to retain your integrity. There is nothing worse than a person who does not practise what he preaches, not just from the point of view of demoralising others or looking ridiculous, but also because it undermines your own will-power. Your inner conscience knows that you are not being true to yourself, and the one person you should never try to fool is yourself. This will cause internal confusion and the effect of that will be a loss of will-power.

BEING SUCCESSFUL

There is a fantastic magic within us all, but of all the qualities we have, the most precious is our will-power. This will help us to overcome all problems. Loneliness, despair, bereavement, even poverty, both material and emotional, can be conquered if we have the will to do so. It is quite fantastic to meet those people who live in dire conditions but are still able to radiate a certain joy and concern for others when their own circumstances are much worse. This is a characteristic of true greatness, at the root of which lies the power of will. The following exercise will help you develop the power of your will and become successful in achieving your goals.

EXERCISE TWENTY-TWO:
The Secret of Success

For this exercise you need to select a particular ambition of yours. It should be something you wish to achieve which does not interfere in any way with the well-being of others and is not primarily for personal gain. It should be a mark of attainment such as musical ability, sportsmanship, public speaking and so on. It could be the ability to mix better socially by becoming less shy or indeed toning down an excessively extrovert nature. It could be the ability to serve others more effectively, or something specific such as becoming a healing presence when you are in the company of others. Whatever it is, you should select this goal before you start the exercise.

You should sit down and prepare yourself in the usual way, with harmonious breathing. Make sure you are relaxed, but with your spine erect, and practise the following creative visualisation. Imagine yourself doing the very thing which is your selected goal. Do not involve other specific individuals in this visualisation, though if your goal is public speaking, for example, you can imagine a general audience without any faces you recognise. As you do this you will probably find that your mind presents certain obstacles. This is where the positive thinking comes in—you have to overcome these obstacles. If you find yourself thinking, 'I could never really do this', change that thought into 'I will learn to do this'. If you find yourself thinking, 'It's easy to do sitting here, but I am not up to it in real life', say 'I am going to be able to do this in real life'. Do not ever lie to yourself by saying, 'I can do this'; always phrase your positive thoughts in the future: 'I will . . .', 'I am going to . . .' and so on.

You may find that your subconscious mind resists this positive change so strongly that you catch yourself thinking the whole exercise absurd. That is the very best time to carry on, because then you can exercise your will-power to overcome this negativity by the very act of continuing. Always remember that these changes do not take place overnight—you will have to work at it. But all the time you are manifesting your will-power, and ultimately you must succeed.

Will-power is at its most effective when it is co-ordinated with the highest part of your mind, your superconscious aspect. The journey into supermind is a journey beyond the normal conscious state of awareness into a state of higher inspiration and intuitive awareness. When you start to cultivate these higher states, you find there are various degrees of higher consciousness. It is at this stage that you are moving from a state of doing into a state of being. You start to become attuned to life as a whole and realise that in reality you are one with all creation.

Most of those who are active in supporting ecological causes do so because they are concerned about the state of the environment. They do not wish to leave a terrible mess to their children and grandchildren. But as you become more attuned to higher mind you are no longer concerned just for future generations of humans, but also for the planet. You become aware that there is a life in all things.

You also become increasingly aware of the interrelationship between all levels of existence and that what affects one affects another. It is no longer good enough to have concepts of living and dying as entirely separate. The physical body dies, but life continues. If you contaminate the physical world, that will have repercussions on the mind belt of the planet at all levels. There is no escape into heaven or nirvana, which are descriptions only of highly elevated states of consciousness—states I personally have never attained. They are goals along the way, but they are not ways of getting out of our responsibilities to the present, as some monks and sannyasins have believed. What we do now affects our body and the energy field around us until we change it. All life exists in a multitude of levels of mind, operating on different levels of frequency but completely interconnected. This is not so much a philosophy as something you start to realise by becoming more highly attuned. It is a realisation which is liberating and at the same time gives you a fantastic sense of what can potentially be achieved with the right degree of motivation. You realise that virtually whatever you set your sights on is attainable, sooner or later.

ONENESS WITH THE WHOLE

Probably the most universally acknowledged goal is the quest for happiness, but it has to be a lasting happiness. Fleeting moments of happiness take on an elusive quality, as though it is something beyond your grasp. It is a state of being which can be cultivated, but it must come from within. It is no good practising escapism, because sooner or later you will come down to Earth with a bump. It has to be real and ever-present. Of course nobody is going to be happy all the time; if they were they would be selfish and sooner or later their happiness would come to an end. After all, a selfish person suffers the most because he feels his personal losses and difficulties much more than an unselfish person. No, if you are aware of the suffering and problems on Earth, you cannot and should not be happy all the time. But there should be an ever-present, inner part of your being that you can draw on, which knows happiness. And this happiness or inner joy can only come from reality, from a recognition of your own identity as a part of a great whole. The following is a beautiful exercise you can perform, which will give you a feeling of being an integral part of a great cosmic whole.

EXERCISE TWENTY-THREE:
Contemplation on the Cosmic Whole

This exercise can bring you great benefits, especially of a spiritual nature. It can lead to higher states of consciousness and a greater awareness of your own place in the cosmic whole. Again, sit with your eyes closed and practise harmonious breathing. Then perform the following creative visualisation. Imagine the universe of stars and planets all arranged with a perfect symmetry, shining brightly against a purple backcloth. You can see those stars as symbols of hope, light and continuity. They never falter, they always shine. They represent a visual divine will of ever-moving manifestation. They are constant beacons of illumination.

Then turn, in your mind's eye, to yourself, a tiny, apparently insignificant speck of dust in the cosmic whole and yet a living being with all the capacity of human endeavour—to think, to feel, to build, to serve. Then try to feel the same sense of continuity, of constant illumination that you have realised about the ever-shining stars and planets in God's firmament. You too can shine on through life without deviating from the light of inner will. Then try to feel a sense of oneness, that even though you are apparently insignificant you have a place in this glorious cosmic whole.

This exercise should not be practised too regularly but, like Exercise Eight (p. 78), should be kept as a special practice to be performed when you wholeheartedly want to do it, giving it your full concentration and all your feeling. Then it will really work for you and, if done correctly, you will find this very uplifting and inspiring. It will bring a deep sense of lasting joy to you.

The ultimate goal of all exercises in supermind is to discover your real self. All the different levels of higher consciousness are really steps towards this knowledge of your true identity. It is like a kaleidoscope of different colours which change before your gaze, as your true nature reveals itself. Others liken it to peeling away layers of a fruit in order to get to the core. Whichever analogy you use, it is an exciting journey of discovery around which whole movements have been built, to teach and guide on this journey. It is a completely natural quest to know yourself, regarded by cultures as diverse as ancient Greece, India, Tibet and China as the key to all wisdom, because it was believed by schools of wisdom in all these nations that if you truly know yourself, you know all things.

DEGREES OF MEDITATION

Swami Sivananda, an advanced yogi and one of the foremost experts on higher mind in the twentieth century, spoke about different degrees of realisation achieved through meditation.

He referred to them as forms of *samadhi*, the Sanskrit word for the deepest meditative states. In the first stage, called *samprajnata samadhi*, he said, there are still subtle mental impressions present—in other words you have not attained the ultimate state which is devoid of all mental impressions. You are in a state of being in which you become one with whatever you meditate upon.

He divided this first state into four separate kinds. The first, *savitarka*, is the perception of an object at all levels, including the sound of the word for this object, the meaning of the word and the form of the object. If you take this far enough, he said, you can know all about this object and its relationship to time and space. The second, *savichara*, is a meditation on the subtle elements connected with the object, including the energy field or aura which surrounds it and the vibrations emitted by or through the object. The third, *sananda*, is a meditation on the mind of the object. Even a physical object has a thought form behind it, it is a result of mind. At this level you start to know all about the object, virtually from the inside. The fourth kind is *asmita* in which you move beyond the physical form, subtle emanations or even mind of the object and become one with its very essence—you virtually merge with its identity. You do not know it so much as become one with it and merge in Nature.

Of course all these states of consciousness have to be experienced. They sound bland when described theoretically. They are said to be accompanied by a sense of peace and elation which has never been experienced before by the practitioner in any field of life. Unlike material pleasures, these experiences have a lasting quality which is yours forever, and that is why the yogis willingly forfeited all forms of physical indulgence. They said that nothing could compare with the bliss which comes from deep meditation.

There is a second state, says Sivananda, beyond *samprajnata* and its various kinds, which is known as *asamprajnata*. In this form of *samadhi* there are no mental impressions whatsoever— not even the impression of oneness—you just are. This is the ultimate state of consciousness, which is beyond mental impulse and is entered by pure, natural will. There is nothing beyond this and, in the Buddhist view, through entering this highest form of superconscious awareness or Nirvana, you break free from the wheel of rebirth. You then live an existence beyond the limitations of physical life and death. You have journeyed so far into supermind that you are no longer bound by physical laws.

It is not only Buddhists who have this concept of breaking free from a purely physical existence into higher, heavenly spheres. There are those who claim to have visited these spheres or to have been visited by those who inhabit them, either mentally or physically. All the religions and most mystical schools have been based upon a belief in contact with higher beings in one form or another, and it is essential to strip away the myths and superstitions which have shrouded so many different versions of what is really a consistent and uniform human belief in contacts with heavenly beings from higher spheres of existence.

14
Heavenly Spheres of Existence

*

Many of the experiences of higher consciousness reported through history have been connected with contacts with higher spheres or realms of existence. While I am not advocating that you should attempt to make such contacts deliberately, and there are no practical exercises given in this chapter to do so, the book would be incomplete without some explanation of these happenings which have been experienced by so many. In your journey to supermind, you may have such an experience—indeed you may already have done so. It is vitally important to understand what is happening, though not necessarily something you should seek. The best way for these things to happen is naturally, as you experience deeper levels of awareness.

CONTACT WITH HIGHER REALMS

It is absolutely vital to discriminate carefully when hearing claims of experiences of higher realm contact. Some are genuine, many definitely are not. They can be deluded, imaginary experiences or in some cases may be caused by hallucinogenic drugs or other substances. There are also cases of deliberate hoaxers who exploit the gullible into believing they are in contact with higher beings of one kind or another and receive money from them in return for a so-called personal message. Invariably these messages are obviously fake to anyone but the person concerned, who feels flattered to have had such a personal message from such a 'high source'.

But after discounting these false claims, there is still a large body of contacts with higher spheres which I believe to be genuine. Indeed many of them form the basis of world religions and are believed by millions, though with different dogmas attached to their interpretation. If you strip away the different dogmas you find remarkable similarities between these religious claims, as you do with mystical groups of various kinds. They all believe that their most advanced leaders were able to attain a rapport with spiritual beings.

The two main methods for contacting heavenly spheres of existence are either some form of heightened mental condition, trance or visionary state, or leaving the physical body in an ethereal state. In the first case, I am not referring to a typical seance where a trance medium gains contact with a deceased relative. This cannot remotely be described as an experience of supermind, though some spiritualists would have you believe it is. It comes under the category of psychic experiences, which I covered in my previous book. I am referring only to those who claim to receive elevated communications from a high source which imbues them with enlightened knowledge or awareness.

OUT-OF-BODY EXPERIENCES

There are now many cases of people claiming near death experiences. Typically they were on an operating table undergoing surgery when they technically died for a few moments before being revived by the surgeon and attendants. They describe themselves leaving the body and floating above it for a few moments, when they see in front of them a long white tunnel. At the other end of the tunnel are white-clad figures. Sometimes these will be relatives who have died before them, or they will be described as angelic beings or spirit guides. Usually the person experiences a great feeling of joy and freedom, and sometimes hesitates before returning back to the body again when it is revived. These are typical involuntary out-of-the-body experiences, which are happening all the time.

Others report leaving their bodies as they go to sleep and looking down on the physical body in bed. Sometimes they panic and immediately return to the body. There are those who have developed the ability deliberately to leave their physical body in what is termed as their astral body. I, for one, have done this and it can be the most exhilarating experience providing you go with it and do not develop any anxiety about the state you are in.

HIGHER BEINGS

But there are other types of experience reported throughout history, which give a far deeper insight into the heavenly spheres of existence. According to a Buddhist text known as the *Anguttara Nikaya*, the Lord Buddha taught:

There will be a time, O monks, when this world comes to an end. And at that time, beings are generally reborn in the Heaven of the Radiant Dieties. There they lie, made of mind, feeding on joy, radiating light from themselves, traversing the skies, living in glory and thus they remain for a very long time. When the world comes to an end, O monks, these Radiant Deities rank as the Highest, but even for the Radiant Deities, change takes place, transformation takes place.

This concept of illuminated beings free of the physical world, living in realms of mind, has much in common with mystical concepts of higher spheres of existence around this Earth, inhabited by elevated souls who are not physically incarnate. The Buddhists called these realms *Deva Lokas*—happy celestial abodes.

Some of history's most inspired thinkers have claimed contact with higher beings. For example, Xenophon tells us that Socrates claimed that 'intimations were given him by a God'. The Theosophists talked in the nineteenth century of Ascended Masters living in retreats around the world, inside mountains such as the Himalayas, who had made contact with their leading figurehead, Madame Helena Blavatsky. These Ascended Masters, all members of The Great White Brotherhood, were described as living in physical bodies but not being limited to the physical world. They could inhabit whichever plane of existence they choose at any particular time. This suggests an ability to control matter by regarding it purely as a frequency energy zone which, with the right knowledge and ability, can be altered. Such an ability is a supreme demonstration of mind power.

The most famous demonstration of reconstituting matter in the physical form was the Resurrection of Jesus. Some Christians cannot live with this concept and are modifying their beliefs to discount the Resurrection as historical fact. It does not fit in with their materialistic concepts, so they are removing it from the dogma of their religion by seeing it as purely symbolic. And yet it is not the only reported case of resurrection. Paramhansa Yogananda, in his book *Autobiography of a Yogi*, gives a beautiful but extraordinary account of this. A devoted student of yoga made a pilgrimage to the Himalayas to find the greatest of all yogis on Earth, the Lord Babaji, a Master who was held in the highest reverence and had reputedly been on Earth in the same body for thousands of years. The student came upon the Lord Babaji, approached him and asked to become his student. As a test which would surely deter all but the most devout in faith, the Lord Babaji instructed him to jump off the edge of the mountain to certain death below, if he wished to become his follower. This outstanding student was so sure of his goal that he did indeed jump and, according to Yogananda, was immediately resurrected, having passed the test set for him. He then became a student of the Lord Babaji.

HIGHER LIFE IN THE COSMOS

Nowadays, rather than looking to Masters of the East, many people look into space for demonstrations of supermind and, according to numerous reports, they certainly find them. Only a concept of higher mind can explain some of the demonstrations performed by visitors from other worlds. If you only believe in the physical and have no concept of higher frequencies of existence, you will repudiate the very idea of inhabited planets anywhere near us, certainly in this solar system. But if you realise that life can exist on Earth in spheres above the physical, then the same is certainly true of Mars, Venus, Jupiter and any other planet.

One of the most interesting UFO reports I received as an investigator of the subject was released by the Soviet agency, T.A.S.S., in 1989 as part of their newfound policy of *Glasnost*. It concerned the landing of a spacecraft in front of many witnesses in a park in a town called Voronezh. It left indentations in the ground and, according to some reports, a mineral sample which was not known on Earth at that time. These were physical clues, but there was another one which interested me more. A boy in the crowd was apparently very frightened and started to cry. A space intelligence who had emerged from the craft pointed what appeared to be a gun at the boy who then immediately disappeared. When the spacecraft left the boy reappeared. Here was a far more interesting demonstration than indentations in the ground or mineral samples, because it suggests a technical control over matter which is far removed from anything we understand, scientifically at least, on Earth—surely an indication that there are different spheres or frequencies of existence.

In case you are wondering whether I have crossed the line and moved into the territory of fiction, I assure you I have not. This was an official government release by an agency which was responsible for the most serious and important news releases to the world. The fact that some of the press could not take it as seriously as news about agricultural policy or nuclear disarmament is a reflection only on their prejudices. Indeed a representative of T.A.S.S. informed me at the time how disappointed he was by the puerile reactions of some Western news agencies to this factually based incident. Those who have seen UFOs, and particularly those who have seen them disappear and reappear, will know how significant this is—not just to the case for life on other planets, but also the immensity of mind energy potential. If these beings can harness such powers as these, then our science is surely on the wrong track in sticking purely to its physical parameters.

The concept of extraterrestrial life on higher spheres is not new at all. We see it in old religious texts such as the Hindu *Ramayana*, where gods travel in celestial vehicles, and the Judaeo-Christian Bible, where variously described aerial objects transport and guide spiritual leaders and prophets. Homer also referred to a time in ancient Greece when the sky dwellers visited the heroes of old. More recently the prominent mystic Emanuel Swedenborg claimed contact with such Beings. Born in 1688 in Stockholm, Swedenborg was to become an outstanding scholar and a most versatile figure in Swedish and European culture. All who knew him attested to his outstanding mental powers. As a relatively young man, he produced books on such diverse subjects as chemistry, metallurgy, astronomy, navigation, dock embankments and mining. He also became an expert in natural philosophy, mathematics and theology and was actively involved in politics as a member of Sweden's House of Nobles. But, in my view, one of the most interesting of all his many works was called *Earths in the Universe*, in which he claimed to hold discourse with the inhabitants, spirits and angels who dwell on other planets, including many of those in this solar system. The communicators visited him, he said, but not in physical form. Their essential message was one of a love, harmony and co-operation far in advance of this world. In order to avoid ridicule, Swedenborg initially published this work anonymously.

Some things change slowly. Even today it is hard sometimes to get such a straightforward and important matter as higher life on other planets discussed seriously. Nowadays there are many claims about such contacts, but none compares with the forty-year, completely consistent claim made by Dr King. Even those who disbelieve his claims to be in touch with higher interplanetary beings in this solar system have to admit that he is the world's most longstanding and completely dedicated proponent of heavenly spheres of existence not only on Earth but, even more so, beyond it. I would go farther than that, but at the very least, he is worth investigating.

LIFE ON MANY LEVELS

When you realise that we are surrounded by life on different levels, you have a much broader approach to all life. You become more at one with the universe as a whole and your part in it. Five hundred years ago, Western man believed the Earth was the centre of the solar system. There was no concept of greater planetary bodies. Today some still try to cling to the idea that we are the only inhabited planet, even though astronomy on a purely physical level shows this to be extremely unlikely. Now, as we move into the new millennium, metaphysical concepts of higher life forms are accepted by an increasing number of people. These are not angels who need wings to fly, but angelic beings who can fly on thought alone— just as you can when you leave the body in an astral state. And these changing views bring a change to your consciousness. They liberate the mind to travel into supermind.

There may come a time when you yourself experience a vision of these higher spheres around this Earth or when you are visited by a being from a higher plane of existence on this planet. Having done countless radio phone-ins on this subject, I am personally amazed at just how many people are having such experiences. If you do, do not panic, but regard it as another part of your discovery of higher mind. Some yogis say we should disregard contacts with such visitors; some mediums become obsessed with them. I would not recommend either approach. If this happens to you, discriminate carefully, learn from it and travel onwards along the road which leads you to your own becoming—when you will unlock your inner powers and know its true meaning.

15

Unlock Your Inner Powers

*

There have been numerous examples, from all cultures, creeds and races, of people manifesting their inner powers of realisation. In the nineteenth century, the Poet Laureate of Great Britain, Alfred, Lord Tennyson, used to silently repeat his own name and experienced a higher state of consciousness by doing so. He wrote: 'A kind of waking trance—this for lack of a better word—I have frequently had, quite up from boyhood, when I have been all alone. This has come upon me through repeating my own name to myself silently, til all at once . . . individuality itself seemed to dissolve and fade away into a boundless thing, and this, not a confused state but the clearest, the surest of the surest, utterly beyond words.' As I mentioned earlier, William Wordsworth used to describe the state of bliss he enjoyed which enveloped him with a feeling of complete oneness with nature and all life. Ralph Waldo Emerson, the American writer and philosopher, also experienced elevated states of consciousness.

ENLIGHTENMENT

Certainly in higher states of consciousness you can experience this feeling of oneness and universality. It is no longer a theory to believe that there is a divine presence in all things—you virtually start to feel and experience it. A feeling of love envelops you for all creatures, including inanimate objects. You look at everything in a different light, as though the sun has come up, illuminating mundane existence. What seemed to you before to be haphazard and random now has a sense of order. The harmony that the Greek philosopher Pythagoras spoke of, both in relation to the cosmos and the sounds which pervade all life, can start to live within you almost as if you had a tangible contact with a mysterious force behind creation.

In higher states of consciousness, what you are really doing is not just altering the state of your mind or indeed the speed of the brain waves emitted through your brain, but more importantly than either of these, you have raised your own personal vibrations onto a higher frequency of existence. As science advances, concepts like this are coming to the fore. Already there is a return in some new fields of scientific research to the principles of quantum physics rather than the theory of relativity. The essence of quantum physics is that energy is related to frequency rather than energy being related to mass, as in Einstein's theory of relativity. Although, of course, it is far more complex than this, the essence of the concept of quantum physics is closer to metaphysical thinking for this reason alone. As I have stressed, frequency is more important in determining evolution than mass or matter. It is the frequency of vibration you are on, not just on a physical level but on a metaphysical level, that determines your state of awareness.

Enlightenment is a state of being. According to Dr King's book, *The Nine Freedoms*, all mental energies within the individual are then transmuted on a deep level of inspiration and high intuition. Enlightenment is something which enfolds you. A wise person is not necessarily an intellectual. He will think deeply and feel deeply and have vast experience, but he will not calculate and deduce his observations in a purely intellectual way. His wisdom will come from a natural sense of awareness which results from the experiences he has had and is reflected in the vibration of his being. The way to attain or indeed contact the higher powers is to raise your vibrations. The Master Aetherius has made the controversial statement that if a person could raise her vibrations to the correct level, she could even tune in to the thought pattern of intelligent life forms now inhabiting other planets. As described in the previous chapter, existence on the other planets does not necessarily manifest on the same level of frequency as it does on this Earth. Of course that opens up a massive debate about interplanetary life, but whatever your beliefs on this matter, the principle is one of tuning in to higher mind,.

TELEPATHY

To prove that you can tune in to the thought emanations of another person, the best method is the practice of telepathy or the transference of thought energy between two people. This is something you may have done without realising it. You think something and then someone repeats the exact words you just thought, too accurately to be a coincidence. This is a common example of thought transference. Or someone comes into your mind for no apparent reason, you phone her and find that she needs your help and was thinking about you, but hesitated to call for one reason or another. This is another example of telepathy: you tuned in to her mental request for help, even though she did not physically carry it through. Telepathy is something you can develop and here are two simple exercises you can use to do this.

EXERCISE TWENTY-FOUR:
Telepathy for Two People

Ideally you will need to get together with someone whom you hardly know or preferably do not know at all. He should be sympathetic to the exercise you are both going to perform and as keen as you to develop telepathic ability. This works very well in courses where there are people who have never met before but are joined in their desire to learn about the higher aspects of life. The old practice of shaking hands is more than a social custom: it has a metaphysical purpose based on the fact that in the palms of the hands there are psychic channels through which natural energies flow. When two people shake hands they are transferring these energies, which should be conditioned with mutual love and respect from one to another.

To do this exercise, sit down and shake the right hand of the other person, palm against palm, but instead of moving the hands up and down, hold them very still and both visualise white light passing from one to the other. Try to feel a great sense of impersonal love for the person you are doing this with, and hold it for about thirty seconds. After thirty seconds, remove your hand and just sit still, observing the thoughts and feelings which come into your mind. Make a note of them if they are significant. Ignore fleeting thoughts which just disappear and never return. If something stays with you, returns to you or gives you a very definite feeling, then note it.

After a few minutes of doing this you can start asking each other questions. For example, if a picture of a boat on a river comes very strongly to you, ask the person whether he has a boat on a river or is planning to have one soon. Some of the things which come to you may seem irrelevant, but nevertheless, talk them out with the person. This is not a test so much as an experiment and you can help each other and be quite relaxed about it.

You may be surprised to find that you pick up something very specific, such as a name which you could not possibly have known, which does apply to this person. If so, note the feeling and the thought you had when this name came to you. That is the feeling you want to be able to recognise on future occasions. Although this seems a trial and error method, it gives you good practical experience. You will then find that you start to recognise the feelings within you which are genuine telepathy and the difference between them and a haphazard wandering of the imagination, or thoughts just passing through the brain.

This very simple practice can be very enjoyable as well as educational, but is at its most exciting when you start to get definite results. It is quite amazing how accurate you can be with this. If you are not successful on the first occasion, do not worry at all; just try again and gradually you should start to get some results.

EXERCISE TWENTY-FIVE:
Telepathy for a Group

This is best done when you are in a group of people. Two of you should step out of the group, preferably a male and a female, to get the right energetic balance, and choose something very general to think about. This can be as basic as water or fire or it might be something like books or trees. Try to make it something positive but general. Then the two people should focus their concentration upon the chosen subject to the exclusion of all else. If it is trees, they do not think about one tree, but about all sorts of trees and forests and the different situations in which trees exist. Or if it is books, they might think of a whole range of different kinds of books. Whatever they choose, they must focus intensely on this for two or three minutes.

During this time the remainder of the group will try to be as receptive as possible. To do this, the shoulders should be relaxed, the eyes closed and they should practise rhythmic breathing for a few minutes before starting. Then they observe what thoughts and feelings go through their minds while they focus on the two people who are concentrating on the subject. The results may be very specific—for example, they might think of a particular tree they know at the end of their garden, or somebody in a religious frame of mind might think about the Bible, rather than books in general—but they just note which thoughts come to them and recur or stay throughout the concentration being performed by the other two.

After a few minutes have elapsed, the two people then ask the others to mention anything that was very strong and came to mind. Again, you may be surprised to find how accurate the results of this exercise can be.

If you become really good at these exercises, you can practise over a distance by prearranging a time for one of you to send out a thought and the other to receive it. You will find that you are able to develop a link with particular people. Twins are very good at doing this together, as are people who are closely connected with each other, such as husband and wife. You should identify the feelings and thoughts which came to you when you were successful. By remembering these you will be able to tune in more and more in the future and ignore those wandering thoughts which were just coming through the brain for no particular reason. With practice you can hone your skills and become extremely accurate at telepathy.

One of the most positive examples of telepathy is the practice of prayer. Again, I say this without drawing upon any particular creed or denomination, because it is something which crosses them all. In fact atheists have been known to pray fervently when crisis struck their lives. It is a natural, instinctive thing to do. But what is really taking place when you pray? Simply a transference of thought. It may be an English prayer to a Christian God or it may be a Sanskrit *mantra*, a Hebrew chant, a Moslem prayer or a mystical invocation. In all cases you are summoning energies through the power of thought to be used in the way you prescribe mentally. It is not so much the meaning of the words which is important, though words do have a mental power in themselves, but far more the motivating impetus you feel when you offer the prayer. Your thoughts and feelings are directed outwards through the prayer in the form of energy. Both prayer and mantra are potent systems to develop your own mind powers effectively and bring about positive change.

THE ULTIMATE STATES OF CONSCIOUSNESS

All the methods I have recommended and taught in this book will culminate ultimately in your journey into supermind. Along the way you will unlock many powers—great mental clarity, a deeper perception, the ability to gain intuitive knowledge about people and things, telepathy, greater inspiration, a sense of oneness, a more directed purpose in life and the inner joy this brings. In the final analysis, it is up to you how far you take it. But when you consider the highest states of consciousness, you have to make very definite changes if you want to go so far. It is not something which everyone would choose to do, and according to Eastern philosophy it can take many incarnations to be ready for these.

Before experiencing even a fairly high state of consciousness, you will be in a state of peace which envelops the whole of your being. This is very pleasant but it is not something which should lull you into a false sense of self-satisfaction. There are those who make the mistake of thinking that this state of deep peace is the final state they have been seeking and are content to leave it at that. However, it is only a step on the way to unlocking your inner powers. The Yogis say that before you can remove the mental obstacles to deep realisation, which they called 'seeds', it is necessary to fry those seeds. One of the symptoms of 'frying the seeds' is this very pleasant, peaceful state which you can enjoy. While it is necessary and can be beneficial, it is not the final goal and you need to be alert and active and persevere if you wish to enter higher states of being.

Some teachers, especially Zen teachers, would be quite severe in the way they treated their students, to ensure that they did not get lulled into staying in this peaceful, non-active state of being. They would tap their students with a cane or use even more severe measures to keep them alert, awake and always striving for the pursuit of higher realisation.

The revered Tibetan Master, Marpa, went farther. He put his chosen student, Milarepa, who was to become an enlightened adept, through severe tests of endurance and faith. It is said that he privately wept at the suffering of his most talented disciple—even wielding a staff in Milarepa's direction more than once. Of course, Milarepa was free to leave, but he had chosen to follow Marpa and having done so had to take whatever his Master determined was necessary. At one point he was bricked into a cave, as was customary in those days, and did not know if and when he would be let out. It was solely at the discretion of Marpa.

This kind of obedience to a teacher is unfashionable nowadays. Westerners see it as undignified to undergo strict discipline and obedience except in certain contexts such as the military where it is seen to be expedient and effective. It can also be effective in the pursuit of enlightenment, providing the teacher knows exactly what he is doing. Marpa did, and eventually his much loved disciple did indeed attain great powers of higher consciousness.

There is a great mystery about this relationship between teacher and advanced disciple on the quest for enlightenment. On the face of it, it can appear to be a severe relationship, but only because the teacher is intent on speeding up the evolution of his disciple as fast as he can, and the disciple in his turn has a deep love for the teacher and, it should be remembered, is a volunteer. Fashionable or not, it is an age-old method used in many different cultures with great success.

But there is sometimes another, deeper factor at work when the teacher is a Master and that is the manipulation of Karma. I mentioned the Karmic Law earlier in relation to mind energy being returned to you in kind, whether good, bad or indifferent. Some mystics believe that an advanced person who has achieved the highest levels of superconscious awareness can take Karma for others to speed up their evolution. In order to balance this, it is necessary for the person concerned to repay Karma by demonstrating not only his complete faith, but if necessary to make sacrifices for the Master who is helping him in this way. In the case of Milarepa, his complete obedience to Marpa, even when it seemed 'unfair', earned him the right to receive initiations of great wisdom and power from Marpa at a later date. He was said to have climbed the Himalayas in only a cotton robe during a severe snowstorm and endured it by the powers he had gained as a disciple of Marpa. More importantly than this, he became enlightened and his name is revered to this very day.

It is believed that some Masters did indeed take Karma for others. By taking on severe illnesses, or even dying, they assumed negative Karma which was not really their due, and thereby helped others who would otherwise have borne this Karma. This would be described, in the Christian Church, as 'dying for their sins'.

These are advanced concepts which, it must be stressed, only apply to those extremely rare individuals who have not only entered the highest known states of consciousness, but have mastered them and decided to go about other work for the benefit of their followers and humanity as a whole. This does not and will not apply to the vast majority of us throughout our lifetime.

Let's not kid ourselves that we have progressed farther than we really have. All the great Masters of history who have been revered for their higher knowledge have demonstrated in their lives complete, self-sacrificing dedication to their goal. It has not been a hobby, or something they have to fit in during a free weekend. Mostly they have advocated complete celibacy as an essential prerequisite for the most advanced states. Many of them have renounced wealth, family life and the basic pleasures of life.

I say this not to advocate that you do the same. On the contrary, it is far more important nowadays, in my view, to get involved in human affairs rather than completely detaching from civilisation, and while this is easier in some ways, it is more difficult in others. It is certainly more complicated, which is one reason the yogis turned away from it. They disliked complexity and always sought the simple truths, in which there was, of course, great wisdom. But though our lives may be more complex and demanding, it is still necessary to make the same degree of sacrifice in other ways if we want to go all the way on this path, because sacrifice, just like joy, is an essential part of the journey—to discover that which is beyond mind, you first have to free yourself of all that is below this.

I realise that this may not sound like a tempting proposition and it is not really meant to. It is all a question of choice. Many will not want to go that far, or may not feel able to do so at this time. Some will see this as a definite goal. But the book would be incomplete if I did not mention the possibility—a possibility I for one have not yet attained.

The ultimate state of being on Earth has been called by many names, probably the most common of which is cosmic consciousness. Some yogis called it seedless *samadhi*. It is a state of being which is even beyond mind, when the consciousness is merged in timeless static space where thinking ceases and being begins. Being here now is the only reality, according to those few who have genuinely attained this state of complete oneness with all creation.

In these higher states of supermind it is said that you start to realise the nature of your true identity. 'I am that I am,' says the Old Testament, and many Sanskrit mantras, in their very advanced mystical language, say the same thing. But it is one thing to think this, quite another to realise it. Two students were sitting discussing their Zen masters. One talked euphorically about how his master could stand on one side of a river and impress his thoughts on a blank piece of paper held by a student on the other side. The other student mused for a while at this story and said that his master could do something even greater: if he slept, for instance, he slept and if he ate, he ate. In other words, the most astounding feat possible is to live in the NOW, and to live fully the experience you are going through, whatever it may be.

An old Eastern story concerns two men who hoped to break the cycle of rebirth by attaining freedom. They both approached a great sage, Narada, and the first, who had been meditating for a long time, said, 'How many lives have I got before I am ready to escape rebirth?' 'Four lives,' replied the sage. He was bitterly disappointed in view of his lengthy meditations. The other then asked the sage the same question. 'How many lives have I got?' 'As many as the leaves on that tree,' replied the sage. 'Is that all?' said the man joyfully. 'That's marvellous,' and he immediately attained freedom from rebirth. This story was taught to illustrate the vital importance of a joyful, non-attached attitude to speeding up your evolution.

All this talk of *samadhi*, Nirvana and cosmic consciousness reminds me just how much I still have to learn and how far I still have to travel. As the great sage Lao Tzu said, 'Much speech leads inevitably to silence.' As with speaking, so with writing . . .

Bibliography

*

Abrahamson, Charles, *The Holy Mountains of the World*, The Aetherius Society, 1994.

Besant, Annie, *Thought Power, Its Control and Culture*, The Theosophical Publishing House, 1920.

Besant, Annie, and Leadbeater, C. W., *Thought Forms*, The Theosophical Publishing House, 1925.

Burke, Richard Maurice, *Cosmic Consciousness*, E. P. Dutton & Co., 1969.

The Dhammapada, Penguin Books, 1973.

Evans-Wentz, W. Y., *Tibet's Great Yogi Milarepa*, Oxford University Press, 1969.

King, George, *Contact Your Higher Self Through Yoga*, The Aetherius Society, 1955.

King, George, *The Nine Freedoms*, The Aetherius Society, 1963.

King, George, *Personal Development, Metaphysical Lessons and Cosmic Wisdom Cassette Lectures*, The Aetherius Society, 1973.

Lao Tzu, *Tao Te Ching*, Penguin Books, 1963.

Ouseley, S. G. J., *Colour Meditations*, L. N. Fowler & Co., 1949.

Pirsig, Robert M., *Zen and the Art of Motorcycle Maintenance*, Corgi Books, 1976.

Proto, Louis, *Meditation for Everybody*, Penguin Books, 1991.

Schul, Bill, *The Psychic Power of Animals*, Coronet Books, 1978.

Shastri, Hari Prasad, *Meditation, its Theory and Practice*, Shanti Sadan, 1936.

Shine, Betty, *Mind Magic: The Key to the Universe*, Corgi Books, 1992.

Sivananda, Swami, *Raja Yoga*, Yoga Vedanta Forest Academy, 1971.

Swedenborg, Emanuel, *Earths in the Universe*, The Swedenborg Society, 1970.

Vande, Wetering, *The Empty Mirror*, Routledge & Kegan Paul, 1973.

Vivekananda, Swami, *Raja Yoga*, Advaita Ashrama, Himalayas, 1970.

Yogananda, Paramhansa, *Autobiography of a Yogi*, Rider & Co., 1950.

Zukav, Gary, *The Dancing Wu Li Masters*, Bantam Books, 1980.

If you would like to receive further information about personal instructional courses or publications on the power of your mind, you are advised to contact:

The Aetherius Society,
757 Fulham Road,
London sw6 5uu.

Tel: 0171-736 4187

Index